Gifted or Just Plain Smart?

Previous titles by Audrey M. Quinlan

A Complete Guide to Rubrics: Assessment Made Easy for Teachers, K–College (2006)

A Complete Guide to Rubrics: Assessment Made Easy for Teachers, K–College, 2nd Edition (2011)

Gifted or Just Plain Smart?

Teaching the 99th Percentile Made Easier

Audrey M. Quinlan

ROWMAN & LITTLEFIELD
Lanham • Boulder • New York • London

Published by Rowman & Littlefield
A wholly owned subsidiary of The Rowman & Littlefield Publishing Group, Inc.
4501 Forbes Boulevard, Suite 200, Lanham, Maryland 20706
www.rowman.com

Unit A, Whitacre Mews, 26-34 Stannary Street, London SE11 4AB

British Library Cataloguing in Publication Information Available

Library of Congress Cataloging-in-Publication Data Available

ISBN 978-1-4758-3114-6 (cloth : alk. paper)
ISBN 978-1-4758-3116-0 (pbk. : alk. paper)
ISBN 978-1-4758-3117-7 (electronic)

♾™ The paper used in this publication meets the minimum requirements of American
National Standard for Information Sciences—Permanence of Paper for Printed Library
Materials, ANSI/NISO Z39.48-1992.

Printed in the United States of America

To Tara and Dan

who planted the seeds for this book.

Table of Contents

Acknowledgements

This book would not have been possible without the contributions and input of a variety of talented educators. These include my colleagues at Seton Hill University, who responded positively to my call for reviewing comments. These generous professors include: Dr. Kathy Harris, Dr. Mary Monsour, and Dr. Jennifer Suppo. Gratitude to Mrs. Bernadette Mendish for supplying "leads" with documentation that extended across the nation. To Carolyn K., Director of the Hoagies' Gifted Education Page, and to Mrs. Amy Skoff, teacher, guidance counselor, and doctoral candidate, my appreciation for close reading and honest feedback.

Teachers and administrators from a variety of school districts throughout the nation provided interview information for this book. A special thank you to the gifted education team of Norwin School District: Dr. Connie DeMore Savine, Mrs. Paula Giran, and Ms. Ciminy St.Clair, who enthusiastically shared time, talent, and experiences. And to Assistant Principal Lisa Banasick, thank you for opening that door!

Parents, grandparents, aunts, uncles, and students revealed stories that made this book come alive. Since most of you requested to be anonymous, I will respect your privacy—but you know who you are! My graduate students at Seton Hill also provided excellent feedback, examples, and encouragement. They recognized the need for this book long before I did.

I am also grateful to the folks at Rowman-Littlefield, especially Tom Koerner, who took a chance on a rookie writer many years ago and continued to encourage me throughout this process.

My husband, Tim, deserves more than gratitude for listening, reading, supporting, helping me find the humor, and for picking up many take-out dinners.

Preface

"Being gifted in schools today is not necessarily a positive experience. Gifted students and their parents experience a lot of rejection from an educational system in which conformity is valued ..." (Winebrenner, 2012, p. 11).

Some of you who are reading this were probably identified as gifted somewhere in your educational life. Others of you were probably friends with (or are parents, aunts, uncles of) students who were in the gifted and talented programs in elementary schools, while others of you may have little idea of the intricacies and politics of gifted education. My personal experiences with gifted education have been mostly positive. Unfortunately, in my research for this book, I have found that Winebrenner's statement is accurate. There are teachers and administrators who willingly accept making accommodations for students with disabilities. However, some of these same individuals reject the notion that accommodations are required for students who are gifted.

I have been teaching in a graduate-level course in gifted education for over ten years. Because of my personal experiences, I advocated for the course to be added to the college catalog. This book is the result of my ongoing search for a textbook. It is also the reason for the "Food for Thought" sections at the conclusion of each chapter. These are activities and reflections that I have used in my course.

As I was writing this preface, I received an email promoting a new book touted as a complete guide to special education. I took the time to click on the table of contents and sample chapters. There is absolutely no mention of gifted students. It is no wonder that pre-service teachers are surprised to see "gifted" under the umbrella of special education.

Whatever your personal experience with gifted education, this book will provide an overview of some of the controversies and issues that face teachers from elementary through high school who are including gifted students in their regular classrooms. It will also provide support, strategies, and some humor for all stakeholders—parents included.

It is my hope that upon completion of this book, parents and students will find the help they need; administrators will be able to hire the best folks to develop gifted education (see the checklist in Chapter 7), and teachers will not be counted among those educators whom Winebrenner considers responsible for the rejection of gifted students and their parents.

Introduction

Gifted or Just Plain Smart? Teaching the 99th Percentile Made Easier is designed so that each chapter can stand alone and readers can select which chapters meet their specific needs. All chapters begin with a connecting quote and end with a summary of the topic and a section of "Food for Thought." These concluding suggestions offer reflection activities that can be used in teacher preparation courses or for program workshops. With nine chapters, the book is easily incorporated into a shortened semester class or workshop on gifted education.

The first two chapters offer foundational background knowledge. They provide history and theoretical basis along with an introduction to some of the controversy and negative attitudes on gifted education. Chapter 1 provides a brief history along with federal and state definitions of gifted education. Chapter 2 focuses on scholarly research and findings, various definitions of intelligence related to identifying gifted students, and government positions.

If you need immediate help with a gifted classroom or your own gifted child, begin with Chapter 3 on "Myths, Truths, and Characteristics of Gifted Students." This chapter will highlight some of the preconceived myths and stereotypes you may encounter. Chapters 4 and 5 are geared to educators, but parents will also find them worthwhile. They deal with legal issues, teaching strategies, tips, and information on unique populations of gifted students. Chapter 6, "Assessment Issues," will be of interest to teachers, administrators, and parents. This chapter on evaluation of students and programs includes a section of questions parents should ask when visiting a school.

Chapter 7 on "Teachers of Gifted Students" should be beneficial to administrators and college professors. Included is a listing of the preferred characteristics of successful teachers of gifted students along with state requirements and national standards. Chapter 8 gives the reader an "ear" on advice and comments from experienced educators, parents, and students. The final chapter provides samples and links to worthwhile resources (including some humor) for use in teaching or parenting gifted students.

Chapter One

History and Definitions of Gifted Education

"You don't have the moral right to hold one child back to make another child feel better."

Stephanie Tolan, Children's Author and Gifted Education Advocate

When a group of teachers was asked when they believed gifted education was first noted in the United States, the speculation ranged from the 1920s (after World War I), the 1940s (after World War II), and even to the 1950s (after Sputnik). These guesses were all logical since major historical events have often affected education policy. However, these teachers were surprised to learn that the recognition of the need for gifted education can be traced back to the years shortly after the Civil War. This chapter presents the history of gifted education in the United States and provides federal and state definitions that are often used as a basis for identifying students.

A BRIEF HISTORY OF GIFTED EDUCATION

In order to understand the current situation of gifted education in the United States, it is helpful to know its history. The first recorded verification of a school system in the United States addressing gifted education is listed as 1868 when the Superintendent of Schools for St. Louis, MO, William Torrey Harris, using the label "gifted students," insisted that students who demonstrated high aptitude be challenged beyond existing curriculum in St. Louis schools.

This was followed closely by the 1869 study of British Sir Francis Galton with evidence from his study that intelligence is hereditary. However, it was

1

not until 1901 that the first school focusing on gifted education was created in Worcester, MA (Haggarty, 2013; National Association for Gifted Children (NAGC), n.d.a.).

Although the criteria used for admittance to the Worcester school in 1901 is not recorded, it was during this time that the Binet Intelligence Test was translated into English and brought to the United States with much fanfare by Henry Goddard. However, it was the "Father of Gifted Education," Lewis Terman, who adapted Goddard's work and published the Stanford-Binet Intelligence Scale in 1916. Items measured on the Stanford-Binet included *memory, judgment, reasoning, comprehension, and the ability to pay attention* (Hearne & Maurer, 2000).

As the teachers noted in the opening paragraph, the ensuing World War I brought the U.S. military into the education field by using intelligence testing with military recruits in 1917. However, it took about ten years for the first textbook addressing gifted education, *Gifted Children: Their Nature and Nurture*, to be authored in 1926 by Leta Hollingworth, known as the "Mother of Gifted Education" (Haggarty, 2013; Olson, n.d.; National Association for Gifted Children (NAGC), n.d.a.).

The title of Hollingworth's textbook revealed that she disagreed with Terman concerning the role of environment and education in developing intelligence. While Terman focused solely on the inherited aspect of intelligence, Hollingworth's interest in nurturing gifted children produced a wider focus on gifted education to include environment and opportunity—especially in the classroom (Barbaro, n.d.). Her work opened the door for gifted education in schools.

FEDERAL DEFINITION OF GIFTED STUDENTS

Thirty years later, the launch of Sputnik by the Russians in 1957 resulted in an increase in funding for gifted education in the United States. By the 1970s, all fifty states had programs in place to identify gifted children in elementary grades (Haggarty, 2013; National Association for Gifted Children (NAGC), n.d.a.). The 1972 Marland Report to Congress led to the first official federal definition for gifted education. This definition provided the basis for the official definition used by the U.S. Department of Education (DoED). The U.S. federal definition of gifted and talented students is as follows:

> The term "gifted and talented" when used in respect to students, children, or youth means students, children, or youth who give evidence of high performance capability in areas such as intellectual, creative, artistic, or leadership capacity, or in specific academic fields, and who require services or activities

not ordinarily provided by the school in order to fully develop such capabilities. (U.S. Department of Education, 2004, p. 388, definition 22)

The federal definition is not without conflict. This definition has been described as being too limiting, too much in favor of the wealthy and educated (see Elitism in Chapter 2), and even too generous. It should be noted that in the original Marland definition, *psychomotor* was included as a gifted trait, but it was eliminated in subsequent definitions (McClellan, 1985; National Association for Gifted Children (NAGC), n.d.a.).

When psychologists and educators were surveyed on the Marland definition, eighty percent agreed with keeping the currently listed selected traits in the definition. However, only about half of the experts wanted to keep *psychomotor ability* in the definition; a smaller group unsuccessfully suggested adding *social adeptness* to the definition (Martinson, 1975). The result of this think tank and of that survey is the federal definition as listed above.

OTHER DEFINITIONS

Although the U.S. Department of Education definition from 1972 does not mention Intelligence Quotient (I.Q.), these scores remain as a key indicator of identifying gifted students for many school districts. One definition, dating to 1991, uses the term "asynchronous development." This term usually refers to students whose mental capacities develop ahead of chronological age. That is, their physical, emotional, and social development is out of "sync" with their mental capabilities. This definition aligns with the popular indicator of I.Q. The I.Q. scores are indexed to age, with 100 as the average. For example, a 5-year-old who gives answers characteristic of a ten-year-old would have an I.Q. of 200 (Kamenetz, 2015).

The 1991 definition was created by a group of parents and educators who met in Columbus, OH, in 1991. Known as the Columbus Group Definition, it reads,

"Giftedness is asynchronous development in which advanced cognitive abilities and heightened intensity combine to create inner experiences and awareness that are qualitatively different from the norm. This asynchrony increases with higher intellectual capacity. The uniqueness of the gifted renders them particularly vulnerable and requires modifications in parenting, teaching and counseling in order for them to develop optimally" (Morelock, 1992; Silverman, 2007, para. 5).

This definition using "asynchronous development" is compatible with the gifted philosophies of both Terman and Hollingworth. Hollingworth used an I.Q. of 170 to define profoundly gifted (Barbaro, n.d.), while Terman's scale developed the original notion of I.Q. and proposed this scale for classifying I.Q. scores:

- Over 140—Genius or near genius
- 120–140—Very superior intelligence
- 110–119—Superior intelligence
- 90–109—Normal or average intelligence
- 80–89—Dullness
- 70–79—Borderline deficiency
- Under 70—Definite feeble-mindedness (Cherry, 2015a; MENSA, 2015).

School districts often use I.Q. scores of 140 as a determining factor for identifying gifted students. Genius or near-genius I.Q. is considered to begin around 140–145. Less than one-fourth of one percent fall into this category. High designations on the I.Q. scale and scores used to determine areas of giftedness include the following:

- 115–124—Above average
- 125–134—Gifted
- 135–144—Very gifted
- 145–164—Genius
- 165–179—High genius
- 180–200—Highest genius
- Immeasurable Genius: Scores that are 200 and over (Cherry, 2015a; MENSA, 2015).

In terms of the general population,

- 50% of people have I.Q. scores between 90 and 110;
- 2.5% of people are very superior in intelligence (over 130);
- 0.5% of people are near genius or genius (over 140) (Wilderdom, 2005).

Other definitions eliminate the use of I.Q. altogether. Renzulli (1978) simply defines giftedness to be a combination of above-average ability, creativity, and (interestingly) task commitment. Additionally, in the United States, each state has its own definition of what constitutes a "gifted student." The state definitions provide the legal basis for gifted education in each state.

For example, Pennsylvania, where gifted education is mandated and which provides no state funding for gifted education, simply states, "Mentally gifted—Outstanding intellectual and creative ability the development of which requires specifically designed programs or support services, or both, not ordinarily provided in the regular education program" (22 Pennsylvania

Code § 16.1; Davidson Institute, 2016a). There is no reference to I.Q. or to asynchronous development.

However, California, where there is neither mandate nor state funding for gifted education, subscribes to asynchronous development without enumerating I.Q. by using a comparison to chronological peers. Its definition lists these categories:

- intellectual ability;
- creative ability;
- specific academic ability;
- leadership ability;
- exceptionally high scores on achievement tests;
- visual and performing arts talent;
- "any other category which meets the standards set forth in these regulations."

California also declares, "Each district shall use one or more of these categories in identifying pupils as gifted and talented. In all categories, identification of a pupil's extraordinary capability shall be in relation to the pupil's chronological peers" (California Code Regs, Title 5 § 3822, Davidson Institute, 2016a).

The state of Texas (mandated and partially funded) also alludes to asynchronous development without listing I.Q. scores. Its policy states,

> [G]ifted and talented student" means a child or youth who performs at or shows the potential for performing at a remarkably high level of accomplishment when compared to others of the same age, experience, or environment and who: (1) exhibits high performance capability in an intellectual, creative, or artistic area; (2) possesses an unusual capacity for leadership; or 93) excels in a specific academic field. (Texas Education Code Ann. § 29.121; Davidson Institute, 2016a)

The interesting component of the Texas definition is the comparison to similar "experience and/or environment" as listed by Hollingworth back in the 1920s. This phrasing opens the door to identify gifted students who do not have access to the opportunities of higher socio-economic groups (see Chapters 4 and 5).

State definitions of gifted education provide the legal foundation of gifted education programs for each school district in each state. The specific abilities listed in state definitions or policies determine the criteria and the services educators may use to identify and support gifted students. For example, South Carolina specifies services for grades 1–12, Maine considers the top five percent of a school population as *gifted* and the top two percent as *highly gifted*, and Rhode Island's definition as listed grants authority exclusively to the each local district.

However, some states, such as Illinois, Indiana, and Massachusetts, do not even list a state definition. In addition, there are wide discrepancies among states as to whether or not gifted education is mandated and whether or not state funding is available. Thirty-two states mandate gifted education. Four of those thirty-two states—Georgia, Iowa, Mississippi, and Oklahoma—have mandated gifted education *and fully fund* these programs. About half of the states (twenty-three) mandate gifted education and *partially fund* the programs.

The remaining states' policies range from "no mandate and fully funded" to "mandated but not funded." The inconsistency among the states is obvious and can be confusing. Students can be recognized as gifted in one state but would not be recognized as such if their family moved across state lines. (The Davidson Institute website as listed in the references provides information about each state's gifted policy.)

SUMMARY

This chapter has presented a brief history of gifted education in the United States and provided a variety of definitions and criteria of gifted students as used by the U.S. Department of Education and various states.

FOOD FOR THOUGHT

- What criteria should be included in a complete definition of gifted students?
- Reflect on your personal experiences with gifted education from your days in elementary, middle, or high school. Write a brief position paper base on your experiences.
- Find your state's definition of gifted students. Compare and contrast it with the definition used by a neighboring state.

Chapter Two

Theories, Models, Positions, Attitudes, and Controversy

"Intelligence is the ability to adapt to change."

Stephen Hawking (n.d.), Theoretical Physicist

Like the ingredients in a hearty stew, definitions of intelligence and theories of gifted education are often simmered together. Throw in research studies, personal attitudes, and private experiences and the result is a dish of unique flavors. This chapter separates those ingredients.

CURRENT INTELLIGENCE THEORIES

In the previous chapter, theories of measuring intelligence by way of an Intelligence Quotient (I.Q.) were summarized. Building upon the intelligence studies of the nineteenth century, four psychologists of the late twentieth century are recognized for their work in defining intelligence that is *not* based on I.Q. Benjamin Bloom, Robert Sternberg, David Perkins, and Howard Gardner have all published a variety of works and studies that present their individual theories on intelligence. Although intelligence has been greatly studied, multiple definitions continue to provide constant controversy.

However, there is a common thread among these four researchers when defining intelligence. All four agree that intelligence can be defined as ability in three areas: (a) learning, (b) posing problems, and (c) solving problems (Cherry, 2015b; Oregon Technology in Education Council, 2007). Educators interpret these definitions to mean that intelligence can be changed and increased by environmental processes, that is, gifted education programs.

I.Q. Theory

As noted in Chapter 1, I.Q. scores provided the basis for gifted education for many years beginning with Terman's work in 1921. Many school districts still rely on individual I.Q. testing scores to identify students who qualify for gifted programs with each district determining the lowest cutoff score—usually to be within the range of 130–140 (Olszewski-Kubilius, & Thomson, 2013). There has been a recent rebellion to ignore I.Q. and use other criteria and objectives to determine placement in a gifted education program (see Chapter 3).

Bloom's Taxonomy Theory

Cognitive objectives that focus on knowledge are often used to measure intelligence. These objectives were identified and listed in a taxonomy that was created in the 1950s (Quinlan, 2012). Known as *Bloom's Taxonomy*, this list classifies cognitive objectives by the level of thinking skills involved from simple recall, which is the lowest level objective, to the highest levels of thinking skills. The highest levels used in gifted education include analysis, evaluation, and synthesis (Quinlan, 2012).

Sternberg's Triarchic Theory

Sternberg was also a part of the great paradigm shift of the 1980s away from I.Q. His research, when combined with that of Bloom, focused on three types of intelligence: analytic (academic), creative, and practical. Analytic intelligence, or the ability to see unique solutions when problem solving, is the only component of Sternberg's theory that can be adequately measured by psychometric tests (Sternberg, 1997).

Sternberg's second component, creative intelligence, poses that creative task performance improves with familiarity. He described task performance processes in creative intelligence as moving from "novel" to "automatic." Students move from "novice" to "expert" within a range of time—some make this move faster than others. An example would be the music child protégé who plays a musical instrument with early expertise as compared with another child who takes longer but reaches the same level (Sternberg, 1985, 1997).

Sternberg labeled his third intelligence as practical. Practical or "streets smart" intelligence "deals with the mental activity involved in attaining fit to context" (Sternberg, 1985, p. 45). As students adapt, select, and shape experiences, they create a fit with their situations or environments.

An example of this would be young entrepreneurs who, without formal education, create successful technology companies in their garages.

Perkin's Theory of Intelligence

One of the most recent researchers in intelligence theory, David Perkins, presents evidence that intelligence can be enhanced by experiences. Often referred to as "learnable intelligence," researchers continue to focus upon Perkin's three components of all intelligence as *neural, experiential,* and *reflective.* A quick summary of Perkins' work can be the "use it or lose it" characteristic of intelligence (Moursund, 2005). Perkins has more recently delved into the relationship between technology and intelligence, which is a perfect fit with the concept that the experience creates an increase in capability.

Multiple Intelligences Theory

When Howard Gardner introduced his book, *Frames of Mind,* in 1983, he revealed his first full-length statement of his theory of multiple intelligences (M.I.) and listed seven ways that people perceive and understand the world. The original seven intelligences are linguistic, logical/mathematical, musical, spatial, bodily kinesthetic, interpersonal, and intrapersonal. Recent additions are naturalistic and existential (Quinlan, 2012). In this work, Gardner initiated a true paradigm shift by broadening the way educators think of intelligence. Instead of "how smart am I?" it became, "how am I smart?" (Quinlan, 2012).

Many educators quickly jumped on Gardner's M.I. bandwagon that seemed to support the statement that "all children are gifted—in some way." However, supporters of gifted education were quick to realize that the M.I. theory could undermine progress made in gifted education. As Delisle (2005), teacher of gifted students, reminds us in a letter to new teachers, as soon as someone claims that all children are gifted, differentiation and support for gifted education may disappear. Controversy about the validity of M.I. theory remains, with many supporters of gifted education cautioning that full acceptance of M.I. eliminates the need for gifted education (Delisle, 2005; Sousa, 2009).

Three Ring Theory

A fifth theorist, Joseph Renzulli, is known for his *Three Ring Theory* developed in the late 1970s. This theory poses that giftedness is composed of three overlapping "rings" or factors. These three rings are as follows: (a) above average ability, (b) creativity, and (c) task commitment. It is Renzulli's theory that when these three factors overlap and interact, giftedness occurs. In this theory, Renzulli believes that education should work to maximize existing potential of these factors and that by offering opportunities to maximize these factors, more students will be able to function at higher levels.

MODELS OF GIFTED EDUCATION

Although teaching and delivery strategies are described in detail in Chapter 4, delivery models of gifted education tend to be (a) pull out to a resource room or (b) addressing needs within the included classroom, or (c) separate classes. Four researched models are listed below.

Triad Model of Delivery

Based on the Three Ring Theory, Reis and Renzulli (1984) developed the Triad Model which is composed of three levels or types of enrichment. *Type 1* is formed by activities that expose students to a wide variety of careers and topics. Demonstrations, videos, guest speakers, and field trips fall into Type 1 Enrichment. These are often whole school or entire class experiences.

Type 2 activities focus on creative thinking and problem solving with metacognition or learning-to-learn activities and can be either independent or group activities. Using research materials, students plan and implement presentations on assigned curriculum topics in level 2.

Conversely, *Type 3* activities permit the students to self-select areas of personal interest (with teacher approval) and to present projects and evaluate products based on the area of interest. Renzulli's emphasis on task commitment is observed in *Type 3* activities (Reis & Renzulli, 1984; Renzulli, 2005). (See Chapter 4 for detailed information on this model.)

Differentiated Model of Gifted and Talented

Françoys Gagné's (2008) Differentiated Model of Gifted and Talented (DMGT) supports a team-work approach of delivery. This version consists of five components. These are gifts (natural aptitudes), talents (competencies), development opportunities, environment catalysts, and intrapersonal catalysts. This approach supports gifted education with the belief that gifted students are developed by program processes and by peers, teachers, and family (Gagné, 2008).

Munich Model and Actiotope Model

There are two other models that are often mentioned within the framework of gifted education. The Munich Model was developed by Kurt Heller, Christopher Perleth, and Ernst Hany as part of the Munich Longitudinal Study of Giftedness in the 1980s. The assessments for this model focus on four areas: intellectual talents, non-cognitive personality traits, environment issues, and performance areas. The Munich Model is one of the few versions that actually lists and includes athletics (Sousa, 2009).

In the complex Actiotope Model developed by Albert Ziegler in 2005, giftedness is defined as attributions made by scientists and changes as the environment or society changes. In this model, giftedness is recognized when a person (a) wants to do something, (b) possesses the ability to do it, and (c) has the awareness that it can be done. As a system-based action approach, the model emphasizes that the environment (society) must consider the behavior as gifted in order for any giftedness to be acknowledged (Sousa, 2009).

Positions, Attitudes, and Controversy

Although types of acceleration as strategies for gifted students are discussed thoroughly in Chapter 4, a discussion of gifted education research on positions would not be complete without reference to two seminal reports.

In 2004, the Templeton Group released the research report on educational acceleration. This report, *A Nation Deceived: How Schools Hold Back America's Brightest Students* (Colangelo, Assouline, & Gross, 2004), reported that teachers and parents were deceived by myths of acceleration. Because of the belief that acceleration would cause psychological harm, parents and teachers were reluctant to accelerate gifted students to other grade levels.

Ten years later, the follow-up report, *A Nation Empowered: Evidence Trumps the Excuses Holding Back America's Brightest Students* (Assouline, Colangelo, VanTassel-Baska, & Lupkowski-Shoplik, 2015), continues to provide evidence for the support of gifted education and various acceleration strategies (see Chapters 3 and 4 for details on acceleration strategies beyond skipping a grade).

Gifted education has been controversial since its earliest days and remains so today. Politics associated with the 2002 No Child Left Behind Act focused resources on struggling students to help increase test scores. Gifted students who were expected to do well on the mandated standardized testing were often overlooked (Goodkin & Gold, 2007). In addition, attitudes on gifted education in the United States seem to depend upon personal experiences with gifted education. Adding the political component and controversy is inevitable.

Two opposite schools of thought are listed below, although others are certainly viable:

• *The "Elitist" position*. These folks believe that *all* students are gifted. Identifying so-called "*gifted*" students is simply identifying "*privileged*" (or *elitist*) students, playing favorites, and causing disruption and even racism in our schools today.

Some of these attitudes on identifying gifted as simply identifying privileged students are formed in elementary grades. A graduate student, reflecting on his elementary years, wrote,

> I ... agree with having equality for [all] the students, especially when students may feel ignored by observing their peers going to different places to learn. For example, the students in my elementary school labeled as gifted in math and science went on a field trip to the Science Center. The students in my class (including me) felt left out. It would have been nice to get out school for the day (Personal communication, Mr. C., graduate student in education, January 2016).

• The "We're-losing-our-minds" position. This group supports the concept that academically gifted students are unique and should be nurtured as the future of our nation—much as a natural resource. This group endorses identifying gifted students and providing educational resources as support (Delisle, 2005; Peters, Kaufman, Matthews, McBee, & McCoach, 2014; Robinson, 2012).

Interestingly, special education teachers often do not realize that gifted education is component of special education. Formerly identified as "gifted" in elementary grades, Miss E., a special education teacher in an autism support classroom, wrote,

> It is important for educators and parents to understand the different services available to gifted students to ensure their success in the classroom. In a way, I feel that the process of aiding a gifted student is very similar to the process of aiding a special education student. Although these students have different abilities and require different services, they still both require assistance from their schools and educators to ensure that they are reaching their full potential (Personal communication, Miss E., special education teacher and graduate student in education, January 2016).

These are two typical current attitudes that continue to affect gifted education. Both will be revisited in the ensuing chapters.

SUMMARY

This chapter provided an overview of research-based intelligence and gifted education theories, positions, and attitudes. Although many other theories of intelligence and gifted students exist, the models discussed in this chapter are among those that are cited most often in the literature on gifted education (Sousa, 2009).

FOOD FOR THOUGHT

- Think of your current position on M.I. Theory and prepare a list of points for both views.
- Although this chapter presented a limited list of theorists, have fun with the Theorist Matching Exercise at the following link. (Note—different theorists are listed after each correct submission.) http://www.gigers.com/matthias/gifted/activity_intelligence_01.html

Chapter Three

Myths, Truths, and Characteristics of Gifted Students

"We are altogether too easily deceived by the time-worn argument that the gifted student, 'the genius' perhaps, will 'get along somehow' without much teaching."

W. Franklin Jones, PhD, *An Experimental-Critical Study of the Problem of Grading and Promotion* (1912)

From the date of the above quote, it is obvious that misunderstandings about gifted students have been around for over a century. If you have ever watched the TV hit, "Big Bang Theory," you have seen gifted stereotypes in action. On that show, scientists with brilliant minds are portrayed as unpopular and socially inept persons who were tormented in middle school.

Although that scenario contributes to humorous viewing and high ratings, these portrayals are only a few of the untrue stereotypes or myths concerning gifted education that continue today. With over hundred years of misinformation, it is understandable that many of these beliefs are difficult to debunk. This chapter lists some of the most common myths and truths about gifted students along with research-based characteristics of "smart versus gifted."

MYTHS, STEREOTYPES, AND TRUTHS

Some of the most common gifted education myths or stereotypes and the corresponding truths are grouped and listed below.

MYTHS

- Being gifted is just luck of birth and privilege.
- All children are gifted.

TRUTH

Those two myths summarize the view that providing gifted education is simply "elitist" as discussed in the previous chapter. Part of the problem can be attributed to using the word "gifted." Philosophically speaking, many will agree that all children have specific areas in which they can excel—their "gifts." However, *educationally gifted* refers to a school setting where a student has an advanced talent or capacity to learn when compared to others of the same age. Using this criteria, all children are *not* educationally gifted (Coil, 2012; National Association for Gifted Children (NAGC), n.d.b.; Olson, n.d.; Wolpert-Gawron, 2014).

MYTHS

- Gifted students love reading and math and are model students.
- Gifted students get all As.
- Gifted students love school.

TRUTH

While some students identified as gifted fall into these categories, the reality is that many students who are gifted actually do poorly in a traditional classroom setting—often due to boredom or frustration. Others underachieve purposely, especially in middle and high school, in order to fit in with a peer group or to do less work.

A fourth grader realized that if he scored well on the spelling pre-test, he would "qualify" for harder words. Within the first months of school, he began to do poorly on the pre-tests but scored perfects on test day. His mother correctly suspected that he was purposely missing words on pre-test day so that he would not have to study harder words. Building on this, some gifted students lack study skills in middle and high school because in the early grades they never had to study.

Many gifted students know how to "do school" successfully and *are* model students; however, just as many gifted students actually dislike school, are disorganized, ignore assignments, and challenge teachers daily.

MYTHS

- Gifted students do well on standardized tests.
- Giftedness can be measured by Intelligence Quotient (I.Q.) tests.
- There is no need to identify gifted students before third grade.

TRUTH

As discussed in the previous chapters, only analytic intelligence can be measured by psychometric testing. Gifted students often see things a bit differently, often way "out-of-the box." This ability to see truly unique solutions when problem solving can be missed if students are not given the opportunity to explain their reasoning.

An instance of this occurred with a first grader. In looking at a group of drawings, he was asked to circle the one that did not belong. Pictured were a bus, a plane, a truck, and a car. Since three are modes of travel on roads, the so-called correct answer would be the plane—the only one in the air. However, this little guy circled the truck and proudly explained to his teacher, "I have ridden in a bus, a plane, and a car; I have never been in a truck!" Since gifted students often express unique reasoning, without the opportunity to explain their rationales, their responses can be misinterpreted. This type of gifted creativity is often overlooked in testing.

Although many gifted students score in the ninety-ninth percentile, it also has been determined that tests can be culturally biased and may reflect environment and exposure more than giftedness (Coil, 2014). An example of this was illustrated when a parent recalled a testing event.

When her seven-year-old described the psychologist-administered test for a gifted program, the child reported that she was told sentences and asked to tell if they made sense or were silly.

Upon further inquiry, the child described one silly sentence about a man who put his "trousers on over his head." Because the parent could not recall ever using the word "trousers," she asked her daughter how she knew that was silly. The child replied, "Actually, Grandma calls my slacks 'trousers'!" Without that generational connection (let's hear it for Grandmas), the child probably would not have had that vocabulary understanding.

School districts have a variety of reasons to postpone identification of gifted students before third grade. The reality is that the standards of the National Association of Gifted Children begin with pre-school. Pre-school teachers relate that they have experiences with three-year-olds who can read, count, and do math. When four-year-old Jack who taught himself to read was asked how he knew what those letters were saying, he shrugged and said, "I just figured it out."

And finally, as with all testing cautions, children may have test anxiety, may be feeling ill on test day, or simply may be reading too much into the question.

MYTHS

• Teaching gifted students is easy.
• Teachers challenge all the students, so gifted students will be fine in the general classroom.

TRUTHS

"If I had my choice between having gifted students and having learning support students in my class, I would probably choose the learning support. They are less exhausting" (Ms. W., fourth grade teacher, personal interview, May 23, 2015). She explained that due to the fact that an overwhelming amount of focus is put on helping the low-level learners achieve grade-level success, there is little time and energy left to develop alternative work for the gifted students and other high achievers.

She went on to say that the administration rarely, if ever, holds in-service training for teaching the gifted. As with the majority of the hard-working teachers in this country, she had no training or preparation to teach gifted students. Without state mandates, teachers are not provided the resources needed to teach gifted students (Coil, 2012; National Association for Gifted Children (NAGC), n.d.a.).

MYTHS

• Gifted students will do just fine without support services.
• Gifted students make good peer tutors.
• Gifted children are role models in the classroom.

TRUTHS

Some Elitists believe that students' wealthy parents can provide all that gifted students need. Others believe that gifted students can teach themselves and will do well no matter what happens in the classroom. Research has shown that gifted students require special services to ensure their growth and development. The sad reality is that gifted students at all levels are often the group that learns the least new material in any school year (Coil, 2012; Winebrenner, 2012).

The emphasis on standardized testing from the federal government has not aided gifted students and is one reason these students are not being supported

(Goodkin & Gold, 2007). As one teacher explained, "I know that the bright students will score proficient [on standardized tests], so my focus has to be on the struggling students."

Using gifted children as little teacher assistants to help struggling students does not support their needs. A gifted fifth grade girl was made to help a struggling reader by sitting with her and listening to her read aloud. Although she wanted to be kind, the gifted child was frustrated by wanting to simply read her own book. The struggling reader was embarrassed by having to read to a peer. No one was helped here.

If students have met the grade-level standards, it may seem logical to have them teach others. This faulty logic assumes that teaching struggling students is something gifted children instinctively know how to do. Peer tutoring using gifted students also takes away time that should be used for their own academic development (Coil, 2012; VanTassel-Baska, 2003).

Research has shown that average and below-average students do not see the gifted students in the class as role models. Students usually seek out peers with similar capabilities who are doing well in school. By middle school, being cool is more important than being smart (Coil, 2012).

MYTHS

- Gifted people have poor social and emotional skills.
- Gifted people are physically uncoordinated.
- Acceleration will cause social problems.

TRUTHS

As with the general population, students identified as gifted can be socially inept or gregarious and comfortable in social situations. This one can fool even veteran teachers. At a recent teacher conference, a sixth-grade teacher told the parents of a gifted student that what made their daughter so exceptional was that she was "not a nerd" and was so "popular." The parents wondered what his previous experiences with gifted students—if any—had been.

Most gifted students are emotionally well balanced. However, some areas to watch include the following:

- *Emotional growth is not in harmony with cognitive growth.* Because gifted students' knowledge is at a mature level, one often makes the faulty assumption that emotions are also at that level.
- *Challenges from teachers.* Some teachers—especially in secondary schools—believe that by pushing and challenging students to prove

giftedness, they are helping students to be the best they can be. However, this can backfire to the point of despair and misery.

- *Unwilling to challenge self and earn less than an A.* When the grade is more important than knowledge, students often will opt to take the easy way. One gifted eighth-grader was opposed to having percentages instead of letter grades on the report card. Her reason was that if it said "A," her parents would not know whether it was ninety-three or hundred percent. Listing the percentage would change that.
- *Sensitivity to criticism of self and others.* A sixth grade gifted student, who always loved school, told his parents that he did not want to return to school after the winter break. He revealed that his homeroom teacher was belittling a female who struggled with academics. The parents wisely presented this concern to the school's gifted teacher and the perceived ridicule ended.
- *Self-doubt as to giftedness.* Often referred to as "The Imposter Syndrome," these students attribute their success to luck and not ability. Some will drop out of activities or sports if they are not the best.

In the same vein, physical coordination is not related to giftedness in either direction. Many coaches identify the smart athletes as having excellent coordination along with the ability to play their sports error-free. The gifted "klutz" is just another unsubstantiated stereotype.

Socialization is often used as the excuse for lack of acceleration. The 2004 report *A Nation Deceived* as described in Chapter 2 focused research on the myth that acceleration results in social problems for gifted children. Because most think that acceleration is skipping grades and placing elementary students in college, it is obvious how this myth originated. However, acceleration can occur in many situations with no negative social implications. The bottom line is that acceleration does not cause social dilemmas (see Chapter 4 for details on acceleration strategies).

MYTH

- Children who are learning disabled cannot be gifted.

TRUTH

This is often the most surprising truth concerning gifted education. These children who are both gifted/talented and learning disabled are referred to as GT/LD or as twice exceptional or 2e (Coil, 2012; National Association for Gifted Children, n.d.b., Wolpert-Gawron, 2014). There are three categories of 2e students.

The first group consists of the students who are identified as gifted and their giftedness hides the disability. Next is the group whose severe disability hides the giftedness. The third group is described as the students whose giftedness and disability counteract each other; so neither is recognized (Brody & Mills, 2004; Callard-Szulgit, 2008).

In addition to typical learning disabilities, there can also be emotional, behavioral, or social issues that counteract the giftedness. The appearance of laziness, an inability to focus or concentrate, and evidence of underachieving can be signs of 2e students (Fliess, 2009). The phenomenon of 2e students is discussed in detail in Chapter 5, "Identifying Special Populations of Gifted Students."

GIFTED OR JUST PLAIN SMART?

Teachers everywhere can make use of a simple checklist to distribute to parents who want to know if their child is gifted, creative, or just plain smart. Luckily, these lists have been assembled and have been adapted into one document (see Table 3.1). A word of caution: All twenty areas do not need to be present to meet gifted criteria. However, the list does give teachers and parents a baseline and a perspective to assess student giftedness.

SUMMARY

Even with the help of checklists, discerning between gifted or just plain smart continues to be a challenge for educators and parents. Stereotypes and faulty logic have negatively affected every aspect of gifted education. Without educating teachers concerning these needs and truths, the perception of what gifted students require and can accomplish is constantly distorted (Rockingham County Schools, 2013).

FOOD FOR THOUGHT

Reflect and list the myths or stereotypes with which you have had experience.

- Which corresponding truths about gifted students surprised you?
- What criteria would you add to or delete from the Smart, Gifted, Creative chart?

Table 3.1   Smart, Gifted, or Creative?

SMART (KNOWLEDGEABLE)	GIFTED	CREATIVE
Knows the answer	Asks more questions	Sees exceptions
Interested	Curious	Wonders, "what if…"
Pays attention—focused and alert	Observant but often seems unfocused— Can be multi-tasking	Daydreams
Good ideas	Complex ideas	Wild and silly ideas
Works hard	Can test well with minimum effort	Plays with ideas
Answers questions correctly	Elaborates answers--details	Suggests new ideas or answers
Listens	Strong feelings; opinionated	Often bizarre
Learns easily	Already knows	Asks, "what if…"
Top group	Beyond the group	Can be in the bottom group
6-8 repetitions for mastery	1-2 repetitions for mastery	Asks, "why do we need to memorize …"
Understands ideas and concepts	Constructs abstract but realistic ideas and concepts	Wild ideas
Has a mature sense of humor	Is usually a stage ahead of peers; likes puns, incongruity, and abstract humor. Can become the class clown.	Creates jokes.
Enjoys peers	Prefers older children or adults	Prefers creative peers or works alone
Completes assignments	Initiates projects	Begins multiple projects— often without completion
Receptive	Intense	Independent; unconventional
Enjoys school	Enjoys self-directed learning	Enjoys creating
Technician with expertise	Expert and inventor beyond the field	Inventor
Absorbs information	Manipulates information	Improvises
Good at memorizing	Good at guessing and inferring	Good at brainstorming
Pleased with own learning	Self-critical	Never finished
Gets A's –"Tell me what to do to get the A."	May or may not be grade-motivated	Not motivated by grades

Adapted from: Kingore, 2004; Kotter, 2008; Quinlan, 2012; Szabos, 1989.

Chapter Four

Strategies, Tips, and Delivery

"Children of 140 I.Q. waste half their time [in school]. Those above 170 I.Q. waste practically all their time in school."

L.S. Hollingworth, 1926 (Williams, 2003).

That 1926 quote from the "Mother of Gifted Education," Leta Hollingworth, reveals her insight into the role that classroom environment and opportunity play in meeting the needs of gifted students from kindergarten through high school. Ninety years later, some gifted students are still wasting time in school.

A first grade student, who had taught herself to read at age 3, wasted her time in school by scribbling all over the back of her correctly completed worksheets. Upon inquiry, the parents discovered that the teacher did not permit the child to check out anything from the school library except a picture book. Upon completion of a worksheet, students were to "draw a picture on the back or read their library book." The child took to scribbling in angry frustration.

So what are teachers to do with the children who already know the curriculum? Obviously, caring teachers do not want bored students. There is a cartoon on a Pennsylvania school district's website that illustrates this dilemma. The principal is presenting a new student to the caring teacher saying that the new student is "highly gifted." The teacher replies that since the child already knows the material, the teacher has a special job for him so he will not be bored. The next frame shows the child sweeping the floor!

Although sweeping the floor is an example of the ridiculous, teachers have been known to send the gifted child off as an "assistant teacher" to help sort materials, cut out letters, staple programs, decorate bulletin boards, read to younger children, or (sadly) tutor peers. All of these activities are wasting the academic time of these students.

This chapter presents educational options for teachers and parents of students who are either "just plain smart" or "truly gifted." Various strategies, tips, and models are described.

STRATEGIES

It is estimated that between five and fifteen percent of the school age population is considered to be academically gifted and/or highly talented (Bauer, Benkstein, Pittel, & Koury, n.d.). Although some of these students attend pullout programs for part of the school day, they are usually included in the typical classroom where their needs must be met. Strategies to meet these needs—some with minimal input from the teacher—are listed below. Many of these strategies are simply good teaching and can be adapted for ALL students.

Acceleration Strategies

Acceleration can be defined as "the process of allowing high-ability students to progress through school curriculum at a rate faster than the average. These students are able to cover the same amount of material, with the same degree of understanding as students in a regular classroom setting, but in a shorter timeframe" (Duke Talent Identification Program, 2015b, para.7). A variety of acceleration strategies are described below:

- *Grade Advancement.* With the validated research described in both *A Nation Deceived* (Colangelo et al., 2004) and *A Nation Empowered* (Assouline et al., 2015), teachers and parents can be assured that myths about social problems associated with skipping grades are not supported. Although grade advancement or "skipping grades" is the first thought when educators mention acceleration, acceleration can also be accomplished by other means.
- *Compacting the Curriculum.* In this strategy, students are pre-tested for mastery (usually listed at ninety percent) in specific subjects. Students who have already mastered the content work on alternative activities. This strategy works well with academic subjects that require one correct answer,

which makes it easy to determine who knows the information (Coil, 2008; Winebrenner, 2012).

An example of compacting the curriculum is illustrated by an eighth-grade English teacher. He plans to begin every school year with basic mechanics and usage. He gives a pre-test during the first week of school. If students do well, they spend the nine weeks doing creative writing within the classroom. If he is teaching something they still need (such as quotation marks), they are free to rejoin the class for that skill.

As this teacher learned, accommodating the needs of gifted students does not have to be burdensome. Students scoring high on the pre-test will not have to relearn the information at all. Instead, teachers challenge these students by providing them corresponding opportunities to delve deeper into the topic.

Many times, the teacher does not even have to create the assignment. Students will have many suggestions for their independent projects (Cox, n.d.). Written agreements or *learning contracts* signed by student and teacher are sometimes used when developing plans for independent studies such as curriculum compacting (Coil, 2008; Winebrenner, 2012) (Chapter 9 lists links to learning contract and compacting templates).

- *Advanced Placement (AP) Courses.* A common acceleration strategy is the AP course. High school students have the opportunity to complete college-level courses in English, science, social studies, and math and earn college credit through nationwide testing. Some schools limit enrollment in these courses to students identified as gifted; however, most high schools open these courses to any interested student (Tomlinson, 2008; VanTassel-Baska, 2003).
- *Flexible Pacing or Continuous Progress.* In this strategy, students work at their own pace, usually ahead of their classmates. They continue as long as they are making progress. A student working ahead in the math textbook is an example of this acceleration strategy. This strategy is always closely monitored by the teacher.
- *Dual Enrollment.* Students are enrolled in college courses while still in high school. This can be on-line or even with permission to leave school to attend a local college (Tomlinson, 2008; Virginia Advisory Committee for the Education of the Gifted, 2013).
- *Early Entrance.* Students enter a program or school (often kindergarten or college) earlier than is typical.
- *Subject Acceleration.* This strategy can be described as learning specific content beyond what is typical for the grade level. An example of this

would be a fourth grader going to the fifth grade classroom for math or reading class or a ninth-grader taking AP Calculus.

- *Vertical Enrichment, Leveled Curriculum, Tiered Assignments.* All three terms refer to assignments within the same lesson plan that are structured at varied levels of complexity and depth. Often labeled as "above and beyond" planning, teachers are encouraged to use the higher end of Bloom's Taxonomy when planning lessons and assignments to meet diverse needs. This implies that methods, content, and projects should be more complex, more abstract, and more open-ended (Davidson Institute, 2016b) (see Chapter 6 for a listing of verbs used to create objectives based on Bloom's Taxonomy).

Enrichment and Adaptation Strategies

In addition to the above types of acceleration, other educational enrichment and adaptation strategies are commonly used with gifted students:

- *Independent Projects.* These are individual, in-depth studies of a specific topic. Students usually work with a teacher or mentor to set an appropriate pace for covering work in the subject with a planned culminating project. Learning contracts are often used to delineate objectives (Tomlinson, 2008; VanTassel-Baska, 2003).
- *Academic Competitions.* An Internet search will result in a plethora of team and individual competitions—some nationwide—in a variety of academic areas. Local competitions are often sponsored by area colleges.
- *Technology Resources.* From online classes and researching topics, to team competitions and gaming, technology offers unlimited opportunities for enrichment for all students. WebQuests, online projects, distant learning opportunities, and virtual field trips can be self-paced (Duke Talent Identification Program, 2015b).
- *Using Mentors.* Teachers often contact "experts" in various fields to pair with individual students. The expert mentor can serve as an advisor, counselor, and role model to the student (Duke Talent Identification Program, 2015b). The mentor can serve as a coach for competitions. As one teacher who uses a variety of mentors said, "Gifted kids need tutors, also."
- *Facilitating.* Teachers often feel as though they must always know all the answers. However, especially when working with the gifted, it is preferred that the teacher *guides* and does not demonstrate a "knows-it-all" demeanor. In addition, these students often need less teacher-imposed structure to succeed, so minimal guiding is preferred (Winebrenner, 2012).

Teachers who facilitate learning discover that many times students will find their own answers. A teacher of gifted related how a student whose independent project was on computer programming called her over for help. After a long pause, she was about to admit that his program was beyond her expertise, when he suddenly exclaimed, "Oh, I got it—Thanks." She later told her colleagues, "All I had to do was stand there."

- *Flexible Grouping.* Grouping for gifted students can be by interests and/or ability and can change as interests or topics change. One daily pull-out model has fifth and sixth graders all working on STEM (Science, Technology, Engineering, Math) for four days of the week and on their individual projects on the remaining day. Interest groupings can be arranged in typical classrooms as well as in resource rooms (Tomlinson, 2001; VanTassel-Baska, 2003).
- *Cooperative Groups.* The quandary for classroom teachers is when to place gifted students together in one group and when to use heterogeneous groups. Winebrenner (2012) suggests asking the following three questions:
  o Does the task require input from different types of learning or perspectives?
  o Is the subject matter new for all students?
  o Is it likely that the gifted students will experience real learning rather than simply tutoring the others? (Winebrenner, 2012, p.193).

Answering no to one or more of these questions indicates that the gifted students should be in their own group (Winebrenner, 2012). The remaining students should be grouped heterogeneously with one strong student, one struggling student, and one or two average ability students (Winebrenner, 2012).

- *Cluster Grouping.* The placement of a group of similar-ability students in a regular classroom for all of or a portion of their day is referred to as *Cluster Grouping.* Districts often divide elementary and middle level gifted students among several homerooms to be "fair" to the teachers. However, this is not fair for the students. Research has shown that always being the smartest one in a class can be an excruciating and stressful experience (Winebrenner, 2012).
  One student related, "If I miss even one on a test, everyone says 'oooo.' I hate that." Gifted students thrive in an environment with other gifted students facilitated by a classroom teacher who understands the role of a cluster of gifted students in a heterogeneous classroom (Winebrenner, 2012).
- *Work Stations and Learning Centers.* These areas are designed to enrich a student's interest in a specific content area. Used to supplement curriculum

covered in the classroom, these centers can provide information on a variety of topics not formally covered for all students. A word of caution—teachers must have their resources organized in order for these centers to support independent learning. Beginning without organization is asking for trouble.

- *Student-Centered Decisions with Student and Parent Input.* Accepting that they are all on the same team, teachers must work with the parents and use them to be resource locators. Students and parents both need the opportunity for "choice and voice" when deciding on curricular issues.

- *Goal Setting—Gifted Individualized Education Plan (GIEPs).* According to Section 1414 of Title 16, revised in 2004, the GIEP lists objectives and means of accomplishing them for each gifted student. Although state requirements differ (Zirkle, 2005), a meeting similar to an IEP meeting is usually held. Input is provided by parents, teachers, district representatives, and, if requested, the student. All interested parties meet to decide on the goals and objectives with the means of accomplishing them. The written plan is then agreed to and signed by parents.

  It should be noted that a GIEP does not authorize individual tutors or anything beyond what the district already provides (Zirkle, 2005). For example, if the district does not offer Chinese language classes, a request for such is not legally required to be honored.

- *Learning Contracts.* Although IEPs are required by law for students with special needs, all students can benefit from using written contracts signed by both student and teacher—and sometimes parents—to specify academic or behavior objectives. This written agreement provides structure and guidance (Winebrenner, 2012). A quick Internet search reveals a wide range of learning contract templates that are available to meet a variety of needs from elementary through high school (see Chapter 9 for links to contract templates).

- *Team Teaching.* Whether one is the gifted teacher, the classroom teacher, or a subject teacher, it is wise to work as a team to determine the best educational route for the student. Communication is vital to verify the facts.

A savvy teacher of the gifted in a pull-out program asks classroom teachers to let him know what they are teaching. He then researches true enrichment activities to tie in with the topic that can be used at different levels for the entire class and presents these to the classroom teacher for input. He works closely with the teacher to make it happen. Everyone wins.

TIPS TO TEACHERS FROM TEACHERS

Groups of veteran teachers familiar with working with students who are smart and gifted agree upon the following list of what not to do:

- Do not expect adult-like behavior just because a student has a gifted label. A ten-year-old with a 170 Intelligence Quotient (I.Q.) is still chronologically age 10 with all the developmental characteristics that implies.
- Do not expect strengths in all areas. For example, a math wizard may have horrid writing skills. Academically gifted does not mean strengths in all academic areas; artistically talented does not mean talented in all artistic endeavors.
- Do not lump all gifted students together or believe the myths and stereo-types (see Chapter 3). As with both typical and special needs students, students identified as gifted have a variety of personality and ability differences. The wise teacher will not assume any similar characteristics among the gifted students in the class (Davidson Institute, 2016b). As one experienced teacher advised, "Let go of 'normal.' It just doesn't apply here."
- Do not ask them to do things they already know how to do and expect them to wait for others to learn. Compacting the curriculum works well when students can test out of an area, chapter, unit, or skill (Coil, 2008, 2012; Tomlinson, n.d.).
- Do not ask them to do "more of the same stuff faster" (Tomlinson, n.d., para. 8). Reading more books that are too easy and doing more math problems faster are not challenging strategies. This type of unchallenging work can destroy motivation and interest. Good teaching for gifted learners is paced in response to the student's individual needs (Tomlinson, 2001; VanTassel-Baska, 2003).
- Do not isolate the gifted student at a desk in the back of the room and have him/her move through a subject book alone. Gifted students need peer interaction and social opportunities. Positive interaction with their teachers should be a crucial factor in all children's learning. Subject acceleration can eliminate this isolation.
- Do not assume that a gifted student is self-regulated and can work independently on a research project without any guidance, oversight, or accountability. Sending a student off to a computer lab or library to do research may have surprisingly unpleasant results (Brown, 2015).
- Do not have gifted students "fill time" by completing extra worksheets and puzzles or do classroom chores because they have completed required

tasks. Although "no down time" is an admirable goal, students wasting academic time not learning anything new is a disgrace (Winebrenner, 2012). Planning true learning enrichment and differentiation can be time-consuming, but Internet searches are well worth the time. And often the same project can be used for several years.

- Do not simply give more assignments of the same type when students finish early. Gifted students do appreciate "free" time when the time's activities are geared to areas of their interests.
- Do not penalize gifted students by having them complete all the class work that they missed when attending their gifted pullout program. Teachers often feel that by not having gifted students complete all the class work, they are not being "fair." Fair and equal are not synonyms. This is a form of punishment that borders on cruel, and students often opt out of gifted programs because of this policy (Perin, n.d.; Wormeli, 2006). (see Chapter 6 for fair and equal assessment issues).
- Do not require 100% accuracy before moving on. As the teacher with this power, focus on students' strengths not weaknesses. Be cautious of rebellious students at all levels of ability who will purposely choose not to do a task when told that they "must" (Davidson Institute, 2016b).
- Do not have gifted students spend substantial time in the role of tutor or junior teacher. Although helping peers or reading to younger schoolmates can meet an altruistic need, every minute spent in these endeavors wastes academic time, and as previously discussed, can be painful, frustrating, and embarrassing for all involved.

Of course, there are exceptions to this tip. A teacher recently had her group of middle school gifted students plan STEM lessons to present to the life-skills students in the building. The gifted students experienced valuable real-life scenarios where they had to present and explain hands-on activities to students on the autism spectrum and students with Down syndrome. A surprise result was that the gifted students befriended the students with learning challenges. They all began to sit together at lunch. As anyone who remembers the lunchroom in public middle school will relate, this is huge.

DELIVERY MODELS AND PROGRAMS

Although theoretical models are often described in great detail (see Chapter 2), delivery models for gifted education continue to differ as to grade level and individual school district. The most common models are based on (a) enrichment activities, (b) acceleration strategies, and/or (c) individual adaption of curriculum materials (Olson, n.d.; Tomlinson, 2001; VanTassel-Baska, 2003):

- *Pullout Model.* In this enrichment and adaptation model, the most common model used for elementary grades, students are removed from their typical classrooms for special sessions with a teacher who is assigned to teach gifted students. These resource-room pullout sessions vary between two to six hours per week and are usually small group activities. Depending on numbers, these groups may consist of students of different ages.

Most schools have the resource room located in the student's elementary building and are serviced by a teacher who may travel among buildings. Some districts must bus students in the middle of the day to another school that has the resource room.

Weaknesses of this model include limited time and, depending on the teachers, the lack of integration with the classroom curriculum. If the students travel, that is a loss of instructional time. In addition, in many situations, the gifted students must complete any classroom work that was missed which serves as a penalty for being gifted:

- *Self-contained Gifted Classes.* Some school districts support fulltime-gifted education in a gifted-elementary self-contained classroom. These are often referred to as school-within-a-school models. There are also entire brick and mortar schools for gifted education.
- *Cluster Grouping.* In this more recent model, groups of gifted students are grouped or clustered in the regular education classroom and receive differentiated curriculum for most of the day. Recent research reveals positive results from this model. When planning differentiation for gifted education, there are three questions to ask:
  o SHOULD all kids do it?
  o COULD all kids do it?
  o WOULD all kids want to do it?

If the answer to any of these questions is "yes," then it isn't differentiated (Passow, 1988).

- *Push-in Model.* In this situation, a resource teacher, often a specialist in gifted education, teams with the classroom teacher and visits gifted students in their regular classrooms. This model provides support for the regular classroom teacher, is consistent with the curriculum being studied, and the consulting teacher can present resources for students not identified as gifted.

- *Honors and AP Courses (Acceleration)*. At the middle school and secondary levels, the prevalent model is still the special class, usually in mathematics, science, and English. These honors or AP classes are often offered to all above-average learners in those subject areas. Nearly 14,000 public high schools offer AP courses (Educational Testing, 2014). Gifted identification is not required.
- *International Baccalaureate (IB) Program and Dual Enrollment in College Courses*. These two acceleration models are most prevalent at the high school level. The IB program is still relatively small compared with the AP program in the United States. About 894 U.S. high schools offer the IB diploma (International Baccalaureate, n.d.). Dual enrollment programs offer college credit courses while students are still enrolled in high school or sometimes, in middle school.
- *Triad School-wide Enrichment Model*. This model was designed and developed by Reis and Renzulli (1984) for students who are in full inclusion classrooms. Teachers who have students with varying levels of cognitive ability are familiar with these strategies. Often referred to simply as the "Renzulli Triad Model," it is composed of three levels or types of enrichment that are embraced by the entire school. These three levels to enrich the curriculum for all students are as follows:
  o *Type 1*. This level is composed of activities that expose students to a wide variety of careers and topics. Demonstrations, videos, guest speakers, and field trips fall into *Type 1* Enrichment. These are often whole school or entire class experiences.
  o *Type 2*. Activities at this level focus on creative thinking and problem solving with metacognition or learning-to-learn activities. The activities can be either independent or group activities. Using research materials, students plan and implement presentations on assigned curriculum topics in this level.
  o *Type 3*. These activities permit the students to self-select areas of personal interest (with teacher approval) and to present projects and evaluate products based on the area of interest. There is an emphasis on task commitment and "real-life" problems in *Type 3* activities (Reis & Renzulli, 1984; Renzulli, 2005).

Key features of the Renzulli Triad Model emphasize that all stakeholders—parents, students, staff, teachers, and administrators—must understand and accept the model. Training and orientation programs for all, the formation of school-wide enrichment teams, open communication, flexibility, and ongoing evaluation and monitoring are all required to make the program a success (Reis & Renzulli, 1984; Renzulli, 2005).

Because the Renzulli Triad Model offers enrichment to the entire school population, it eliminates the rally cry of "elitism" and other negative attitudes toward gifted education (Reis & Renzulli, 1984; Renzulli, 2005).

ENVIRONMENT

Whichever model is in place, all teachers must be aware of making the classroom environment a warm and welcoming place for all students. Teachers' attitudes towards diversity will be reflected by their students at all levels. Basic classroom management environmental strategies that are used for all students are also applied for gifted education. These include the following:

- create a room that invites inquiry (pictures, books, areas for music, art, and a variety of materials);
- use thematic instruction to connect content areas;
- make a wide range of materials available;
- arrange for activity centers for self-initiated projects;
- have flexible seating arrangements;
- offer attractive, lesson-related enrichment activity options for students who finish work early;
- vary the atmosphere of the room through music, art and movement;
- allow for flexible grouping;
- encourage choice and voice;
- use brainstorming for suggested activities (Smutny, 2000).

Hollingworth in the 1920s knew that classroom environment and opportunity play an important role in meeting the needs of gifted students from kindergarten through high school. Some fifty years later, another reminder from author Haim Ginott combined teacher tips with environment issues for all students. Reprinted and quoted many times, it was originally written in the 1970s, but it still applies today.

> I have come to a frightening conclusion.
> I am the decisive element in the classroom.
> It is my personal approach that creates the climate.
> It is my daily mood that makes the weather.
> As a teacher, I possess tremendous power to make a child's life miserable or joyous.
> I can be a tool of torture or an instrument of inspiration.

I can humiliate or humor, hurt or heal.
In all situations, it is my response that decides whether a crisis
will be escalated or de-escalated, and a child humanized or de-humanized.

Haim Ginott, author
Teacher and Child, 1976

SUMMARY

This chapter explored the topics of enrichment, acceleration, and adaptation as viewed in gifted education. Lists of strategies, teacher tips, program models, and classroom environment suggestions were provided.

FOOD FOR THOUGHT

- Focus on the three types of enrichment in the Enrichment Triad Model. What is your experience with these types of activities?
- Do a quick audit of a local classroom—or even your own. What evidence of support for gifted students is apparent? What would you add?
- Research activities for differentiation. Apply Passow's three-question test (should, would, could) to each activity to determine authenticity.

Chapter Five

Identifying Special Populations
of Gifted Students

"In a roundabout way she was talking to me. I knew I would never be part of the gifted and talented kids. That much was true. But I was one of the *special* people ... I was also in special ed."

Joey Pigza in *Joey Pigza Swallowed the Key* by Jack Gantos (1998, pp. 68–69).

There are three large special populations of gifted students who are currently still at risk. These three populations are as follows: (a) the wide range of twice-exceptional students, (b) diverse gifted students from lower socio-economic groups, and (c) gifted females (Callard-Szulgit, 2008; Duke Talent Identification Program, 2015a; Olszewski-Kubilius, Subotnik, & Worrell, 2012; Reis, 2002; Winebrenner, 2012). This chapter provides background on these three groups.

TWICE EXCEPTIONAL OR 2E

In the above quote, as fifth grader Joey Pigza sneaks into an assembly limited to students in his school's gifted and talented program, he realizes that he indeed has commonalities with students in the gifted program. Astute teachers reading about Joey will also realize that Joey's vocabulary, creativity, and deep thinking reveal that, in addition to his attention deficit hyperactivity disorder (ADHD) characteristics, Joey's ability is above and beyond the students who are simply "schoolhouse smart."

Joey should be offered an opportunity to enrich his studies, but sadly, his disability label overshadows him, and his giftedness is never recognized. Joey is an example of students who should be identified as *2e—twice*

exceptional. Students who have above-average intelligence and are identified as having one or more disabilities make up this category. These gifted
students have the potential to do well in school, but are not succeeding for
many reasons.

The director of the Hoagies' Gifted Education Page describes this special
population as "Twice Exceptional = Exceptional Squared!" and declares "…
there is as much 'good' as 'bad' in twice exceptional learning styles." She
follows that with "… a list of successful people who have capitalized on their
exceptional learning styles!" (K., Carolyn, 2016, para. 1, p. 36).

Although the phenomenon of students being both learning disabled and
gifted was identified as far back as 1970, the use of the terms *2e* and *Twice
Exceptional* can be traced to a 1981 colloquium at John Hopkins University
(Bracamonte, 2010). With over fifty years of research on 2e issues, also
referred to as GT/LD (gifted talented/learning disabled), many practicing
teachers, including special education teachers, are still surprised to learn the
possibility that their disability-labeled students may also be gifted (Callard-
Szulgit, 2008; Winebrenner, 2012).

The most common exceptionalities associated with 2e include the
following:

- Learning challenges—most often learning difficulty—including dyslexia,
  dysgraphia, dyscalculia;
- Behavioral problems—including oppositional defiant disorder (ODD);
- Attention deficit disorder (with or without hyperactivity);
- Autism;
- Asperger's syndrome.

It is estimated that over 70,000 students in the United States have been
identified as 2e (Bracamonte, 2010). Yet, twice-exceptional students are
among the most frequently under-identified population in our schools (NEA,
2006). In addition, "two to five percent of the gifted population have LDs
[learning disabilities] and two to five percent of students with LDs are gifted"
(Bracamonte, 2010, para. 5).

Three scenarios make it difficult to identify 2e students:

- Students identified as gifted whose *giftedness hides the disability.* Signs of
  the disability may show up later as academic challenges increase. These
  students are often accused of simply being lazy or of not meeting their
  potential when their schoolwork falters.
- Students identified as disabled whose *disability hides the giftedness.*
  Students receive services for the identified disability but not for their gifted

level. However, these students may show exceptional abilities in some areas. Because of this, they have a better chance of being identified.

- Students identified as "average." These are highly intelligent students whose *intelligence and disability mask each other.* These students seem average because their two exceptionalities cancel each other (Brain Balance Achievement Centers, 2016; Callard-Szulgit, 2008; NEA, 2006; Winebrenner, 2012).

IDENTIFYING CHARACTERISTICS OF 2E

Identifying gifted students with other exceptionalities is still difficult. High-functioning students with Asperger's syndrome or students with a physical disability are often the easiest to identify as gifted. The frustrations students (and their parents) experience because of unidentified strengths and disabilities can result in behavioral and social/emotional issues. For some twice-exceptional students, behavior plans become the focus of their interventions. The behaviors are managed, but the underlying disabilities are never addressed (Colorado Department of Education, 2012).

However, what should teachers look for in struggling students with ADHD, dyslexia, dysgraphia, dyscalculia, ODD, or any other exceptionality or challenge? Strengths of these students can be the same as other identified gifted students. Look for more than one of the following:

- excellent vocabulary;
- highly creative;
- resourceful;
- curious;
- imaginative;
- questioning;
- problem-solving ability, shrewd;
- sophisticated sense of humor;
- wide range of interests;
- advanced ideas and opinions;
- special talent, ability, or consuming interest;
- incongruity between expected and actual achievement;
- concurrent evidence of a processing deficit

(Brain Balance Achievement Centers, 2016; Bracamonte, 2010; Colorado Department of Education, 2012; Winebrenner, 2012).

Emotional issues of twice-exceptional students can contribute to blocking success in school. These students who often have expectations of success tend to experience some of the following affective and academic challenges:

- easily frustrated;
- fear of failing and not being able to replicate any successful experiences;
- anger at not being successful;
- poor written expression—content and handwriting;
- highly sensitive to criticism;
- low self-esteem;
- stubborn;
- scheming and needing to control;
- strong opinions;
- argumentative;
- inconsistent academic performance;
- poor organization and study skills;
- inconsistency on standardized assessments;
- difficulty with social skills (Bracamonte, 2010; Brain Balance Achievement Centers, 2016; Colorado, 2012; Strop & Goldman, 2002; Winebrenner, 2012).

Standardized and Intelligence Quotient (I.Q.) tests are often not reliable for 2e students. Some will score at a high level on gifted testing, but usually perform poorly on state standardized tests of individual progress. They often do well on tests of spatial relationships, pattern recognition, verbal understanding, and abstract concepts. They do not do well on rote memorization or processing details (Bracamonte, 2010; Fliess, 2009). Of course, exceptions always exist. One 2e student was identified as gifted because of her speed in processing; however, she needed help with fluency and comprehension.

Their scores may vary greatly between verbal and nonverbal subtests (Winebrenner, 2012). Reading is often below grade level, but these students may have a great deal of interest and information in a specific topic. In addition, look for misbehavior actions that are aimed to distract peers from their perceived incompetence (Winebrenner, 2102).

Service models for 2e students are the same as for other gifted students (see Chapter 4). The exception would be a school or cluster group devoted entirely to students identified as 2e (Callard-Szulgit, 2008). Because difficulty with language arts skills are evident in many 2e students, basic intervention strategies in these reading and writing skills are often necessary (Bracamonte, 2010; Fliess, 2009; Winebrenner, 2012).

As districts continue to identify 2e students at all levels in our schools, teachers are wise to realize that "Twice exceptional children don't need to be 'fixed.' They're not broken. They simply need your guidance as to how best to forge ahead" (Fliess, 2009, para. 10).

DIVERSE GIFTED STUDENTS FROM
UNDER-SERVED POPULATIONS

Federal data from a 2016 school survey reveal "a continuing deep gulf between the educational experiences of traditionally disadvantaged student groups and their peers on a broad range of indicators" (Blad, 2016, para. 1). The "traditionally disadvantaged" are often listed as those students who have limited English proficiency, who are disabled, or who are from minority or low-income backgrounds (National Association for Gifted Children (NAGC), n.d.c.).

Among the items surveyed were advanced high school math and science courses. High schools with higher levels of Black and Latino enrollment were found to be less likely to offer Algebra II, calculus, physics, and chemistry (Blad, 2016; Brown, 2016).

Beyond the advanced high school courses, it was reported that the unequal access for minority students also extended to gifted education classes. In schools where Black and Latino students represent about half the population, only twenty-eight percent of students enrolled in gifted courses are Black or Latino (Brown, 2016; Blad, 2016). This persistent underrepresentation has not changed since the 2012 survey (Blad, 2016).

Reasons for this discrepancy are often focused on identification processes and include the following:

- culturally biased standardized tests;
- unfamiliar idioms and language on the tests;
- teachers do not recognize gifted characteristics in nonproductive students (Freishtat, 2016; Olszewski-Kubilius, Subotnik, & Worrell, 2012).

In addition, "… districts that rely on teacher or parent referrals to identify gifted students tend to under-refer low-income and minority students, because the process is subjective" (Freishtat, 2016, para. 7).

For students of color who are identified as gifted—especially in the upper grades—being in gifted education is "uncool" or "being White" (Olszewski-Kubilius, Subotnik, & Worrell, 2012). An African-American graduate student wrote,

> I agree that some African Americans sell themselves short to keep the persona of being black. The black persona seems to indicate that there are no attempts to better themselves and they settle to be average. For the African-Americans who want to better themselves and achieve higher academia, the black persona may consider this as trying to be white. Therefore, the achievement becomes an embarrassment among their black peers. Personally, I have observed these issues

among my peers, and I shake my head. The conversation should not focus on black or white, because at the end of the day, everyone should be self-motivated to succeed and [should] have determined how to receive the resources to make it happen (T. Cole, graduate student, personal communication, January 2016).

Awareness of the issues has resulted in many districts and states making positive efforts to identify and serve a broader range of exceptional students. These include the following:

- Using local scores in making gifted education decisions. This would enable gifted programs to serve the top one to three percent of students in the community.
- Comparing the tests score to similar demographics and learning opportunities. Students in poverty would be compared to other students in poverty, as would students with English as a second language.
- Beginning the identification process in kindergarten, accumulating the information, and annually reviewing local achievement data to identify students who are making rapid improvement (Freishtat, 2016; Olszewski-Kubilius, Subotnik, & Worrell, 2012).

However, there are still many schools where high-ability students are not receiving any recognition or support services (Brown, 2016; Blad, 2016; National Association for Gifted Children (NAGC), n.d.c.). As the Assistant Secretary for Civil Rights, Catherine Lhamon, stated, "We in this nation do not offer high-rigor coursework to all students across the board" (Brown, 2016, para. 7). Until we do, students will not be reaching their potential.

GENDER ISSUES IN GIFTED EDUCATION

This third group of at-risk students generates much controversy. Research has shown that gifted males and females may feel societal pressures to deny their giftedness to fit into stereotypical molds. Often developing from peer pressure in middle school, this need to confirm can send mixed messages to both groups. Boys are persuaded that to be more masculine, they must deny sensitivity and be athletic; girls are often encouraged to drop math and science for more "feminine" courses (Digest of Gifted Research, 2015; Duke Talent Identification Program, 2015a).

Although males and females both feel pressures, females are often the ones who will drop out of gifted programs. A group of teachers of gifted students recently challenged the idea that gifted females are at risk of being overlooked. As one said, "This is 2016. We have women breaking glass ceilings all over the place—even running for president!" And then, one by one, they began to think of situations where they had witnessed different standards or expectations for females.

One teacher related that the focus in her program was on STEM (Science, Technology, Engineering, Math) projects. More than once, elementary teachers would tell her excitedly that they had a "STEMMY girl" for her program. "They never tell me they have a STEMMY boy. That is just assumed." A middle school science teacher then confessed that she recruits "attractive women" to be guest speakers in her eighth-grade class in order to fight the stereotype that female scientists are all unattractive. "I search for attractive female engineers, pharmacists, and doctors. I never care what the male speakers look like."

Losing gifted females in middle school is still more prevalent than losing their male counterparts. One teacher revealed how a bright middle school girl opted out of his advanced math class with parental blessing because "she would never need it." He could not convince her (or her parents) to stay. Another remembered her own experience as a student. She recalled that she had been in the elementary gifted program but dropped out in middle school. She said, "I really do not remember why I made that decision."

This "middle school malaise" (Kerr & McKay, 2014, p. 144) affects both males and females and can be attributed to environment in conjunction with development. In preschool through grade six, gifted boys and gifted girls are about equal in number. By middle and high school, gifted boys outnumber gifted girls (Comallie-Caplan, 2013).

Research has shown that cultural stereotypes about the roles of women have a strong effect on gifted females denying their giftedness. Some of these stereotypes include the following:

- Self-esteem tied to being pretty and popular.
- The "air-head" mystique: Airheads are "hot" and popular; "Brains" are boring.
- Math stereotype: Girls can't do math; boys can.
- Parent stereotypes—Dads are smart; Moms aren't—they just work hard.
- Competitiveness is unfeminine; girls and women should hide their desire to win and give up.
- Leadership is unfeminine; female leaders are often called "bossy" or "aggressive."
- Perfectionism and risk taking are at odds with each other.
- Pressure not to invest too much time in a long education.
- Mothering metamorphosis; can women continue to be "fire eaters" and mothers?
- Glass ceilings and sticky floors mean women cannot reach the highest levels in business (Kerr & McKay, 2014; Langille, 2003).

These stereotypes continue through adulthood. During her 2016 presidential campaign, Hillary Clinton was accused of being "too ambitious" (Associated Press, 2016, p. A4). "If a guy is described as ambitious, it's a noble attribute ... If a woman is ambitious ... it's a pejorative" (Verveer as cited in Associated Press, 2016, p. A4). In addition to these cultural stereotypes, there are psychological issues. Mary Pipher, author of *Reviving Ophelia*, as cited on the Hoagies' Gifted Education Page (2016) writes,

> Because with boys failure is attributed to external factors and success is attributed to ability, they keep their confidence, even with failure. With girls, it's just the opposite. Because their success is attributed to good luck or hard work and failure to lack of ability, with every failure, girls' confidence is eroded. All this works in subtle ways to stop girls from wanting to be astronauts and brain surgeons. Girls can't say why they ditch their dreams; they just "mysteriously" lose interest (Hoagies' Gifted Page, 2016, para. 1).

This view of success being attributed to luck and not ability was identified in 1978 as "the imposter phenomenon" (Reis, 2002). Although this phenomenon is not limited by gender, females who were identified as gifted and were participants in gifted programs continued to deny their intelligence (Kerr & McKay, 2014; Reis, 2002).

Research reveals that gendered educational practices—especially pressure for athletic activities for boys—along with cultural stereotypes and expectations concerning females may have far-reaching outcomes. Academic choices that affect long-term career successes are often related to gender issues, such as women choosing less prestigious universities, less competitive careers, and careers that will accommodate motherhood (Kerr, Vuyk, & Rea, 2012).

Advice to Teachers

Suggestions to help keep gender issues to a minimum for males include being alert to the tendency for boys to "... have low social self-concepts, [be] self-critical and pessimistic, ... to internalize their own concerns, and learn to avoid assistance" (Duke Talent Identification Program, 2006, para. 9). Encouraging extracurricular activities to include volunteer work, or being involved in music, art, drama, or even helping with athletic organizations as a trainer or manager can help. Because young males require positive role models to evaluate conduct, activities with strong mentor possibilities are preferred.

Through high school, girls continue to receive mixed messages about their ability to succeed (Digest of Gifted Research, 2015). Advice to teachers of gifted girls must include an awareness of these stereotypes that are subtly conveyed through media, peer groups, parents, and sadly, even teachers. Although, as women gain more prominence and publicity, it is expected that these negative stereotypes will disappear; however, teachers and parents must continue to make concerted efforts to ensure that all gifted students are not internalizing negative beliefs concerning gender (Digest of Gifted Research, 2015).

Madison Kimrey, age 12, as quoted in Kerr and McKay (2014), instructed teachers to "… help the gifted girls you encounter to be comfortable with and confident in who they are. Providing the most advanced work isn't always as important as providing the right kind of work to help your students discover their own path" (Kerr & McKay, 2014, p. xv).

SUMMARY

This chapter investigated three large populations of gifted students who are currently still at risk of not being identified, encouraged, or included in gifted programs. These are the wide range of twice-exceptional students, diverse gifted students from lower socio-economic groups, and gifted females. Characteristics and stereotypes of each group were delineated with suggestions for meeting unique needs.

FOOD FOR THOUGHT

- Reflect on your personal experiences with the three at-risk populations and list examples of support or nonsupport of the issues discussed.
- From your experience, compare and contrast characteristics of successful male and female leaders/bosses/teachers.
- Research media messages that subtly promote various stereotypes.

Chapter Six

Assessment Issues

"... envisions schooling as an escalator on which students continually progress, rather than a series of stairs, with landings on which advanced learners consistently wait."

Carol Ann Tomlinson

As Tomlinson (n.d.) described what it means to teach gifted students successfully, she compared an escalator to a series of stairs. And she is so right. Too often, our gifted students are losing learning opportunities by waiting on those "landings" and doing puzzles or playing games rather than continuing the upward flow. This is often because teachers are not willing to assess and progress.

Standard 2 of the National Standards in Gifted and Talented Education focuses on assessment. Assessment knowledge is crucial for all teachers. However, teachers of gifted students must also be well informed about individual student identification, the ongoing progress of each student, and program processes (National Association for Gifted Children (NAGC), n.d.d.). This chapter describes those three areas of assessment.

Assessment and testing issues for gifted education fall into three distinct categories:

- Identification of gifted students;
- Assessment of individual students in the gifted programs;
- Assessment of the program.

This chapter provides background for all three areas.

IDENTIFICATION OF GIFTED STUDENTS

As discussed in previous chapters, there is no one sure way to identify a gifted student. Intelligence Quotient (I.Q.) tests, standardized tests provided by various publishers, scores in the ninety-ninth percentile, checklists (see Table 3.1), referrals by parents and teachers, portfolios, accumulated data, case studies, or profiles are all identification tools.

With the passing of the Every Student Succeeds Act (ESSA) in December of 2015, districts are permitted to use multiple measures of student performance. This change in national policy opens the door for districts to be more creative in employing a range of assessment activities that will work for all students of varying abilities (ASCD, 2016).

Case studies and student profiles that identify both strengths and weaknesses are valuable in recognizing gifted students, including special populations as discussed in Chapter 5. Early identification is critical especially for special populations. However, cautions must be observed to ensure that:

- Assessments are equally weighted.
- Best performance is used as an indicator of potential.
- Quantitative scores are comparable.
- Errors in assessments are considered.
- Performance over time is described (Johnsen, 2009).

ASSESSMENT OF INDIVIDUAL STUDENTS IN THE GIFTED PROGRAMS

With identification processes, educators get the yes/no answer to the question as to whether or not the student qualifies for special services. Once students have been identified as qualifying for gifted services, ongoing assessment can help to ensure that students are progressing and that programs are meeting individual needs.

Most gifted students are accustomed to receiving good grades. For many, anything other than an A represents failure. This aim for perfectionism, especially in gifted girls, often means that gifted students are reluctant to take risks or accept challenging activities. Image and ego are often involved (Tomlinson, n.d.).

Dr. Sylvia Rimm, psychologist and author who specializes in working with gifted students, tells us, "The surest path to positive self-esteem is to succeed at something which one perceived would be difficult. Each time we steal a student's struggle, we steal the opportunity for them [sic.] to build self-confidence. They must learn to do hard things to feel good about themselves" Rimm (n.d., para. 1). Teachers who understand this dynamic can help all students to accept challenges and take supported risks (Tomlinson, n.d.).

Rimm's work is supported by Carol Dweck's recent research with mindsets. Working with individual fifth-graders, Dweck used three types of praise at the conclusion of a short test. Students were praised for their intelligence, or for their effort, or simply told they scored well. They were then given a choice of the type of task they wanted next. The two tasks were described as (a) being in their comfort zone where they would make no errors or (b) being challenging where they would make errors but learn something significant (Morehead, 2012).

The majority of students who were praised for intelligence chose the easy task; the majority of students praised for effort chose the hard task where they would learn something. As a follow-up, Dweck gave all students hard problems. The students "praised for intelligence lost their confidence, because if success meant they were smart, struggle meant they weren't" (Dweck as quoted in Morehead, 2012, para. 21). However, the students praised for their process remained secure in their work (Morehead, 2012).

In addition to praising for effort and not for intelligence, strategies to encourage and support risk-taking among all students include the following:

- Reassurance that more challenging work will not lead to lower grades. A parent recently wrote,

  "For me, the most important element was that students should not be penalized for work done at the compacted, or higher, level. It drives me crazy each week when my son passes his spelling pre-test with 100%. He is then given the 'independent speller' word list. He takes a test on these (much harder) words at the end of the week and THAT score is what goes into the grade book. I have argued over and over with his teacher that his spelling grade should be 100%, as that reflects his ability to spell the 3rd grade words. He should not be penalized for improperly spelling words that are two, three, or even four years beyond what the other students in his class are working on. Otherwise, he will eventually learn to intentionally do poorly on the pre-test in order to get the easy 'A' later" (T.K., personal communication, 2014).

- Providing non-graded activities and quizzes. If this has never been done, students may seem skeptical. However, before starting a new topic or skill, teachers are encouraged to give an ungraded quiz to see what all students already know. These informal assessments provide an accurate measure of students' knowledge (Coil, 2008; Cox, n.d.; Winebrenner, 2012).

- Teachers often believe that without the "threat of a grade," students will not do their best. In contrary, students at all levels can feel a sense of relief and new spirit of trying and learning new things when they are assured that no one is "judging."
- Reassurance that they will not have more work than their classmates will. Expecting students to take on an enrichment project in addition to assignments for work already mastered is a sure way to prevent students from attempting new tasks.
- Self-assessment activities provided by the teacher. There are many ways for students to self-assess. Winebrenner (2012) suggests:
  o The "ticket out" strategy where students answer a specific question, list what they learned, or even ask a question or index cards.
  o Personal journals on content where students submit notes about their confidence in specific academic areas.
  o "Give me five" strategy where students indicate their comfort levels with instructed signals of the number of fingers—from the one-finger "I am completely lost" through the five-finger, "I ready for more difficult work."
  o Using rubrics. Opponents of rubrics contend that rubrics stifle creativity, especially in gifted students. They argue that students will submit only the minimum required for the A points. However, teachers of gifted students recognize that a well-constructed rubric that provides a top score for work "beyond expectations" actually encourages creativity. In addition, the rubric blueprint helps the frequent perfectionist gifted students to achieve their best work without undue stress and anxiety (Quinlan, 2012; Winebrenner, 2012).

Tasks that are at the higher levels of Bloom's Taxonomy are appropriate to use for rubric creation for students identified as gifted. Some verbs used as descriptors for these higher level tasks include: *differentiates, applies, creates, revises*, and *generalizes* (see Textbox 6.1).

For example, an analytic rubric to assess critical thinking used in Hawaii Public Schools has the following four areas:

- Applies prior learning experiences to new situations [*generalizes*].
- Considers multiple perspectives [*differentiates*] in analyzing and solving a variety of problems.
- Generates new [*creates*] and creative ideas and approaches to developing solutions.
- Evaluates the effectiveness and ethical considerations of a solution and makes adjustments [*revises*] as needed.

Box 6.1

BLOOM'S TAXONOMY, GENERAL OBJECTIVES, AND VERBS

Category 1: Knowledge/Remembering

- Instructional objectives: Knows/remembers common terms, specific facts, methods and procedures, basic concepts, and principles.
- Verbs used in objectives: *Defines, describes, identifies, labels, locates, lists, names,* and *states.*

Category 2: Comprehension/Understanding

- Instructional objectives: Understands facts and principles; interprets verbal materials, charts, and graphs; estimates future consequences implied in data; and justifies methods and procedures.
- Verbs used in objectives: *Converts, defends, distinguishes, infers, explains, rewrites, paraphrases, gives examples, summarizes, generalizes,* and *translates.*

Category 3: Application/Applying

- Instructional objectives: Applies concepts and principles to new situations; applies laws and theories to practical situations; demonstrates correct usage of a method or procedure.
- Verbs used in objectives: *Changes, computes, discovers, operates, manipulates, uses, modifies, predicts, produces, shows, solves,* and *relates.*

Category 4: Analysis/Analyzing

- Instructional objectives: Recognizes unstated assumptions; recognizes logical fallacies in reasoning; distinguishes between facts and inferences; and analyzes the organizational structure of a work or relevancy of data.
- Verbs used in objectives: *Breaks down, points out, differentiates, distinguishes, discriminates, relates, subdivides, surveys,* and *outlines.*

Category 5: Synthesis/Creating (*Note that in the newer model this category is the highest or sixth level of the taxonomy.*)

- Instructional objectives: Writes a well-organized paper; gives a well-organized speech; composes a creative piece; proposes a plan or a possible solution, integrates learning from different areas into a plan for solving a problem; and formulates a new scheme for classifying ideas.
- Verbs used in objectives: *Categorizes, creates, revises, rearranges, devises, combines, composes, generates, organizes, plans, reconstructs,* and *designs.*

(*continued*)

> **Category 6: Evaluation/Evaluating (*Note that in the newer
> model this category is the fifth level of the taxonomy.)*
>
> • Instructional objectives: Judges the logical consistency of written material; judges
>   the adequacy with which conclusions are supported by data; and judges the value
>   of a work using standards of excellence.
> • Verbs used in objectives: *Appraises, compares, concludes, constricts, criticizes,
>   referees, prioritizes, justifies, interprets, supports,* and *summarizes.*
>
> Source: Quinlan, 2012.

The four grading score areas on the critical thinking rubric range from *Consistently* (4); *Usually* (3); *Sometimes* (2); *Rarely* (1); and *Never* (0) (Hawaii Public Schools, n.d.).

As with most parents, parents of students identified as gifted appreciate the precision and purpose that rubrics provide. As one parent commented after being shown the critical thinking rubric, "Well, that certainly helps to clarify what they [teachers] mean by 'critical thinker' in grade five. This will eliminate many tears—from both of us."

Student-generated rubrics are used with great success, especially with middle and high school students. Within teacher guidelines and approval, the students create their own scoring guides. When students are encouraged to use Bloom's Taxonomy to create their own rubrics, they are invited into the assessment process and the assessment becomes more meaningful. Often students include items that the teachers would not consider; however, these items are vital to them and provide additional insight into their uniqueness (Quinlan, 2012; Tomlinson, n.d.; Winebrenner, 2012).

Veteran teachers of the gifted warn that expecting gifted students to move ahead only when they have mastered at hundred percent accuracy can backfire. Since many use the words "quirky" and "rebellious" to describe the thinking and learning of gifted students, it is the prudent teacher who will realize that *forcing* students who are gifted to attempt risks will not work. Trust may come slowly. As one expert advised, "Give them time to build their, often atrophied, wings in a safe environment" (Davidson Institute, 2016b, para. 14).

PROGRAM ASSESSMENT

Individual ongoing assessments of gifted students differ from typical student assessments in that they should demonstrate advanced and multifaceted learning. Using the data from ongoing assessments is one component of program evaluation (Tomlinson, n.d.; Willard-Holt, n.d.; Winebrenner, 2012).

As previously discussed, programs for gifted education vary from state to state and from district to district and sometimes from school to school. However, some universal indicators of quality can be identified. It has been found that successful programs share the following attributes:

- The program is respected by the community.
- The program is described by students and parents as challenging and valuable.
- There is evidence of student success beyond what would be expected if no program were available.
- There is a sound and stated philosophy that reflects current research and provides a definition of giftedness.
- There is a written guide for student placement.
- A continuum of services is offered.
- Services are integrated into the school day (Callahan, 2010; Willard-Holt, n.d.).

The ultimate question for all stakeholders to ask is, "If students are successful in this program, what will they know, understand, and be able to do that they would not have known, understood, or been able to do had they not been in the program?" (Callahan, 2010, p. 19).

In addition to the above criteria, evaluators of a gifted program should review verification of quality of the following areas. The program should have evidence of the following:

- a specific plan;
- a budget that is adequate;
- involvement of all key stakeholders;
- formative and summative assessment procedures;
- multiple data collection sources;
- assessments that are reliable and valid;
- findings that are both oral and written;
- accommodations for unique circumstances;
- transparency and public access (Purcell & Eckert, n.d.; Willard-Holt, n.d.)

In addition to the above strengths, reviewers agree that common weaknesses in a program usually appear in the curriculum. Common flaws in curricular offerings are as follows:

- *Different but not differentiated.* As listed in Chapter 4, Passow's (1988) three-question test for differentiation is a quick way to validate enrichment activities. Simply asking *should, would, could* questions (see Chapter 4) can help.

- *More fun and games than substantive.* Many teachers believe that any puzzles and games can be considered as enrichment for gifted students. They are not. Passow's (1988) three questions can also be effective here.
- *Not tied to the characteristics specified in the program's gifted definition or to the assessment carried out in the identification process.* Referring back to definitions and assessment results should help to focus activities for gifted students.
- *Tied more to teacher interest than to sound curricular modification.* A change in teachers can precipitate this weakness. Parents of an elementary student whose strength was math were dismayed when their child's new gifted teacher focused all activities on reading, writing, and history. He was losing academic time. Individualized Education Plan (IEPs) and Gifted Individualized Education Plan (GIEPs) should provide specific direction in these situations.
- *Not tied to clear goals either for the immediate or long range.* Again, reviewing the stated philosophy and goals can help a program maintain objectives (Callahan, 2010; Winebrenner, 2012).

WHAT PARENTS NEED TO ASK

Gifted programs must stand up to parent scrutiny as well as to state and district reviewers. Questions for parents to ask along with suggested answers to seek are listed as follows:

- How are students identified? Look for multiple criteria such as written and standardized tests, interviews, teacher recommendation, portfolios, and performance-based assessments. If performance-based assessments are used, ask to see the scoring rubrics.
- What are faculty qualifications? Look for experience with gifted students as well as college-level courses in gifted education and state endorsements or teacher certifications if those are available in your state (see Chapter 7).
- What evidence is available for true differentiation for gifted students? Look for curricular acceleration terms such as "compacting" and "tiered assignments" and the use of pre-tests to place students appropriately.
- After getting the above answers, ask to make an appointment to visit and observe. All quality programs should be transparent and welcome observation (Taibbi, 2015; Willard-Holt, n.d.).

SUMMARY

Expertise about all forms of assessment is critical for educators of students with gifts and talents. The three areas vital to gifted education (identification of students, assessing each student's learning progress, and evaluation of the program) were described. Strategies to encourage supportive risk-taking among gifted students were outlined.

FOOD FOR THOUGHT

- Think of a specific learning unit at any level. Using verbs from Bloom's Taxonomy create three sets of objectives for varying abilities including a gifted student.
- Create or find a scoring rubric for a specific academic area task that defines creativity and risk-taking. How would students use this for self-assessment?
- Looking at Tomlinson's escalator analogy at the beginning of this chapter, think of a personal experience (your own or of someone you know) that reinforces Tomlinson's correlation.
- Reflect upon a personal risk-taking. Does this reflection validate or disprove Rimm's statement of needing difficulties for self-esteem?

Chapter Seven

Teachers of Gifted Students

"Showing up at school already able to read is like showing up at the undertaker's already embalmed; people start worrying about being put out of their jobs."

Florence King, *Reflections in a Jaundiced Eye*

Fortunately, most primary teachers are not threatened with job security when a five-year-old arrives already reading at the fourth grade level. However, many teachers are not equipped to adapt, accommodate, and accelerate curriculum for these early readers. Although it is obvious when a five-year-old reader or math wizard enters school that the child is either "just plain smart" or "truly gifted," there are many times when gifted students arrive in classrooms without their giftedness recognized and, therefore, waste academic time.

Misusing academic time is not limited to gifted students. A recent study reported that, "across the United States, 95 percent of kindergartners tested in the fall demonstrated mastery of counting up to 10, identifying one-digit numbers, and recognizing geometric shapes. Despite this widespread level of proficiency, teachers reported spending an average of 12.7 days per month reteaching this content, a finding negatively associated with student learning" (Peters et al., 2014, p. 34).

STATE REQUIREMENTS FOR EDUCATORS OF GIFTED AND TALENTED STUDENTS

The reality is that whether they were aware of it or not, most teachers, from pre-school through high school, will have had gifted students included in their classes more than once. This group of unaware and unprepared teachers constitutes the first category of how educators fail our gifted students. However, it may not be their fault. Many teachers have had minimal or no training in teaching gifted students (Delisle, 2005; National Association for Gifted Children (NAGC), 2014).

This lack of awareness is not limited to general education teachers. It is commonplace for special education teachers to be surprised that gifted education falls under their special education certification umbrella. These special education teachers "do extraordinary things to help students with learning disabilities be successful. However, when it comes to students who are gifted, some teachers are inflexible and resentful of the behaviors characteristic of being gifted" (Colucci, 2015, para. 5).

Teachers often report that they have had little or no training in the gifted end of the special needs spectrum or information on students who are twice exceptional (see Chapter 5). They simply have never viewed gifted education as part of their area, and the topic was never required by their pre-service programs (Callard-Szulgit, 2008; Delisle, 2005; Winebrenner, 2012).

Many times, these pre-service college programs are simply following their state guidelines, which may make no accommodations for gifted education. In a survey conducted by NAGC, only one state (Nevada) had a *legal requirement* for a separate course in gifted education at the pre-service level. Although twelve states reported that pre-service teacher candidates are required to receive gifted education coursework in teacher preparation programs, there were no statutes or mandates to support the requirement (National Association for Gifted Children (NAGC), 2014). In addition, there were no required distinctions among teaching levels.

"ANY GOOD TEACHER CAN TEACH GIFTED KIDS"

This myth is one reason that states are slow to require college courses in gifted education. At a recent curriculum meeting, a group of administrators questioned the need for a state mandate for requirements for teaching gifted students. Because they believe that teaching gifted students is "easy" and that good teachers "can easily teach any student," these superintendents and principals felt that no other training should be required (Coil, 2012; Szymanski & Shaff, 2013).

However, teacher interviews revealed that most veteran teachers of the gifted report that teaching gifted students "… is the hardest, most challenging, most exhausting … teaching they have ever done," (Coil, 2012, para. 13). To undertake this teaching task without preparation can be an invitation for frustration, fallouts, and ultimate failure.

Although there are still limited requirements for undergraduate pre-service courses, some states are developing post-baccalaureate certificates, degrees, and endorsements. Currently, about half of the states reported having some type of certificate or endorsement available for gifted/talented education. However, within that group, only nineteen states require that educators who are assigned to teach or to administer gifted education programs actually have any credentials in gifted education (National Association for Gifted Children (NAGC), 2014).

Of those nineteen states, twelve states had endorsement or certification requirements and the remaining seven had a variety of listed competencies (National Association for Gifted Children (NAGC), 2014).

Despite an increase in awareness of gifted education, most pre-service college programs offer only one course entitled "Introduction to Students with Exceptional Needs" or something similar. Usually a one-semester offering, this course must contain information on all exceptional needs at all grade levels—PreK–12. It is understandable that gifted education may warrant minimal attention in these programs [see Chapter 9 for a list of "Standards for Teacher Preparation in Gifted Education" developed by The NAGC and the Council for Exceptional Children (CEC)].

As a result, many teachers enter classrooms with little or no training in gifted education (Berman, Schultz, & Weber, 2012). With only a superficial understanding of the characteristics and needs of gifted learners, these teachers depend upon their own preconceived perspectives (see Myths in Chapter 3) of the characteristics of gifted students. Moon and Brighton, as cited in Szymanski and Shaff (2013, p. 3), reported that teachers with misconceptions on giftedness "… were also less likely to identify a gifted student who 'has a lot of energy, may have difficulty remaining in seat, [or] gives unexpected, sometimes smart-aleck' answers."

PREFERRED CHARACTERISTICS
OF TEACHERS OF GIFTED

Because there is no guarantee that teachers have received formal training in gifted education, what else should administrators look for when hiring teachers of gifted students? Following is a checklist compiled from several studies. It should be noted that many of these characteristics are desirable for *ALL* teachers; however, these traits must be highly evident in teachers of gifted:

- high intelligence—for secondary teachers in Advanced Placement (AP) courses, expertise and competency in their certification areas is a given;
- an understanding of and empathy for gifted students from personal experiences—perhaps been gifted themselves;
- a background of academic courses in gifted education;

- positive experiences with gifted programs or students;
- broad knowledge with a wide variety of interests;
- organized, but not necessarily neat;
- sense of humor and comfort with personal strengths and weaknesses;
- originality and creativity in problem solving;
- self-confidence and personal achievement;
- enthusiasm, energy, and drive;
- promotes student independence;
- preference for teaching gifted children;
- comfort with abstract themes and concepts;
- open and flexible—including flexible teaching styles at all levels;
- knowledge of inquiry-based instruction;
- values logical analysis and objectivity;
- understanding of unique characteristics/needs of gifted students to include less practice time and more time with abstract thinking;
- excellent oral and written communication skills;
- good listening skills;
- maturity;
- willingness to work with staff;
- knowledge of assessment and identification issues—including students who are twice exceptional;
- ability to respond to students and to embrace social issues;
- comfortable teaching higher order thinking and research skills;
- comfortable with compacting and differentiating curriculum to meet individual needs;
- willing to model risk-taking (adapted from Heath, 1997; Mills, 2003; Ramsey, 1990; Tomlinson, n.d.; Walden, 2015; Winebrenner, 2012).

RESPONSIBILITIES OF TEACHERS
OF GIFTED STUDENTS

What do the teachers of the gifted actually do? Depending on the grade level and program, job descriptions vary greatly. Some gifted teachers at the elementary level travel to several schools and have caseloads of ninety or more students. High school teachers may be limited to students in AP courses. And teachers of gifted in the middle level may have dedicated resource rooms, may co-teach in support of general education teachers, may teach high-ability groups in academic areas such as math or science, or may be self-contained with students of all abilities.

Generally speaking, any teacher of gifted students should be able to

- advocate for gifted students;
- organize and coordinate enrichment and acceleration activities;
- gather materials to support classroom teachers;
- nurture creativity;
- integrate curriculum;
- communicate effectively with students, parents, and colleagues;
- develop curriculum to meet individual needs;
- provide a safe environment where mistakes and risks are welcomed and supported;
- help students acquire skills;
- model self-evaluation;
- counsel, advise, and encourage leadership;
- present college and career options—especially in secondary schools (adapted from Heath, 1997; Mills, 2003; Ramsey, 1990; Tomlinson, n.d.; Walden, 2015; Winebrenner, 2012).

PROFESSIONAL DEVELOPMENT PROGRAMS AND TEACHER ATTITUDES

There is a word of caution for administrators and others interviewing prospective teachers for gifted programs. While professional development or teacher in-service programs geared to teaching of gifted students may increase understanding of gifted issues, these program often do not lead to support for meeting gifted needs or to a change of a negative attitude (Caldwell, 2012).

The reasons are varied. Negative experiences with gifted programs can stem back to elementary school with current teachers still harboring long-held harmful attitudes toward gifted programs and toward gifted students. Some teachers continued to be intimidated by the intellectual precocity of these students and yet remain supportive of other areas of special education (Caldwell, 2012).

Even with academic work in gifted education, these teachers still cling to bitter feelings. One teacher in a graduate program recalled, "... students who did not excel in the classroom were in the gifted program simply because they did well on their standardized testing. I did not do well on standardized testing, but excelled in the classroom, yet I was not considered gifted." She continued that even in high school honors courses, she did better than those who were "labeled gifted." (Ms. P., personal communication, February 2015).

GIFTED AND TALENTED STANDARDS
FOR ALL TEACHERS

With negative attitudes prevalent, administrators and teacher-educators should keep in mind the following three gifted and talented education competencies for *all* teachers. These guidelines, quoted from the NAGC (2015), are indicated for use in teacher preparation programs as well as for professional development training for teachers already in the classroom:

1. All teachers should understand the issues in definitions, theories, and identification of gifted and talented students, including those [students] from diverse backgrounds.
2. All teachers should recognize the learning differences, developmental milestones and cognitive/affective characteristics of gifted and talented students, including those from diverse backgrounds, and identify their related academic and social-emotional needs.
3. All teachers should understand, plan and implement a range of evidence-based strategies to assess gifted and talented students, to differentiate instruction, content and assignments for them (including use of higher order critical and creative-thinking skills), and to nominate them for advanced programs or acceleration as needed (National Association for Gifted Children (NACG), 2015; Teach.com, 2016).

BUDGET ISSUES

A discussion of hiring teachers for gifted programs would not be complete without a look at budget issues. School districts throughout the nation are forced to make difficult budgetary decisions. Unfortunately, school boards and administrators often make cuts to gifted programs based on the myth that gifted students will do well without support. These cuts frequently eliminate coordinators of gifted programs and/or funding for gifted programs.

Javits Act

The Jacob K. Javits Gifted and Talented Students Education Act of 1988 is the federal education act for gifted and talented education. Named for a senator from New York, the Javits Act provided funding for the National Research Center on the Gifted and Talented, which is run by the University of Connecticut and the University of Virginia. The Center's purpose is to develop best practices in gifted education to identify and serve students with gifts and talents, with a focus on gifted students from low income or minority backgrounds and twice exceptional students (Council for Exceptional Children (CEC), 2013; Estes, n.d.).

Although federal funding for the Javits Act was eliminated in 2011, it was restored in 2014 and has received increases since. The increased funding means that there will be additional competitive research grants and support for the National Research Center on the Gifted and Talented (Estes, n.d.).

ESSA Supporting Gifted Education

In December of 2015, Congress reauthorized the Elementary and Secondary Education Act (ESEA) of 1965. Replacing the controversial No Child Left Behind Act, the new legislation has been tagged as the Every Student Succeeds Act (ESSA) (Conrad, 2016; Islas, 2016).

Four components of Every Student Succeeds Act (ESSA) relevant to gifted education are as follows:

- Title I—ESSA now permits districts to use Title I funds to support gifted and talented learners in poverty.
- Title II—ESSA requires that state Title II applications address issues of identification and instruction of gifted and talented students.
- State and Local Report Cards—ESSA requires districts and states to report student achievement at each achievement level, disaggregated by student group.
- Computer Adaptive State Assessments—Since ESSA permits states to use computer adaptive assessments, data may now be available that indicate mastery above grade-level standards (Conrad, 2016; Islas, 2016).

SUMMARY

This chapter on teachers of gifted students covered the recommended characteristics and qualifications of teachers of gifted students, the varied state requirements of teachers of gifted students, the expectations and standards at each teaching level, teacher attitudes, and professional development. Recent legislation and budget issues that affect hiring practices were also listed.

FOOD FOR THOUGHT

- Using the checklist of desired characteristics of teachers, compose several interview questions that would help interviewers discern specific traits and attitudes needed by teachers of the gifted.
- Research your state's guidelines for teacher preparation programs, certifications, and/or endorsements for teachers of gifted students. Compare those findings to policies in neighboring states.

Chapter Eight

Building on Experience

Voices from the Field

"Experience is that marvelous thing that enables you to recognize a mistake when you make it again."

Franklin P. Jones, American Journalist

When teaching students identified as gifted, educators at all levels benefit from the experiences of others. Although the previous chapters quoted a variety of researchers in the field of gifted education, this chapter focuses on comments and opinions from interviews, blogs, essays, surveys, and journal entries of experienced professors, gifted coordinators, classroom teachers, parents, students, and other experts on gifted education. These "voices from the field" can enhance perspectives on gifted education.

WHAT EDUCATORS OF GIFTED STUDENTS ARE SAYING

Interviews with teachers of gifted students at all levels revealed some common threads. The most often mentioned is the universal lack of preparation to teach gifted students. As one veteran teacher put it, "Unfortunately, many teachers who do not receive training about teaching gifted students believe gifted students are simply really smart kids ... this is perhaps the most exasperating belief a person can have about this complex group of students" (Colucci, 2015, para. 4).

As discussed in Chapter 7, many university professors agree with that statement. Some education professors independently include an objective for gifted education in syllabus planning. One professor of language arts methods at the elementary level specifically includes assignments that have pre-service teachers make hypothetical accommodations for gifted students in unit plans. However, many classroom teachers are still not prepared for what they meet in gifted students.

In a group interview, teachers of gifted students were asked what they wish they had known before taking the job. Knowledge of the variety of characteristics that gifted students exhibit was information they needed. "I wish someone had told me how 'quirky' gifted kids can be. It took me a while to figure that out," said a 12-year veteran teacher of gifted whose elementary caseload is close to a hundred students—all unique!

As others nodded, another added, "More information on twice-exceptionalities is what I needed." Both of these topics—quirkiness and 2e—came together in a comment by an elementary teacher "… being gifted often comes with quirks and eccentricities from having a lot of information passing through your brain at one time … I've become good at spotting 'giftedness' through these quirks. I look for kids who need to talk through everything, kids who have a lot of anxieties and kids whose ability and performance don't match up" (Moran, 2016, para. 2,3).

Another said that as the middle-grade gifted coordinator, she sometimes felt "alone in the building." The group agreed that some of their colleagues think that teaching gifted is easy. "Some of my peers in the classroom still equate 'gifted' with those smart kids who know how to 'do school,' are well-behaved, and do their schoolwork to perfection." Although many educators are well informed about characteristics of gifted students, stereotypes and myths remain. It is sometimes difficult for a classroom teacher to believe that students are gifted if they do not earn all As.

For example, a seventh grade student with emotional and behavior issues including violent outbursts was recently identified as gifted based on Intelligence Quotient (I.Q.) scores. His teacher simply shook his head and said that he did not believe it. "How can he be gifted if he is identified as ED? He can't keep up with the gifted kids!" (Colorado Department of Education, 2012, p. 55). Sadly, this teacher did not realize that giftedness is not a competition. "Keeping up with" others should not be the goal.

High school teachers of Advanced Placement (AP) courses are not sure that their courses should be "open" to any student who wants to take them. An AP calculus teacher related that a student who earned a D in pre-calc, registered for Advanced Calculus. The student promised that he would "work hard" and "do better." Shaking her head, the math teacher reported, "He failed—big time—even after 36 weeks of conferences, recommendations, and offers of tutoring."

And yet, for those who enjoy the "quirkiness," gifted students add much to their teachers' lives. One elementary teacher related that she made a spontaneous joke that went completely over the heads of her fifth-graders. However, she was delighted by the wink of a gifted student who, by that simple wink, let her know that he "got it." With all of his disorganization and reluctance to cooperate, he GOT IT!

Her colleague added, "Most gifted students that I work with love the opportunity to explore new subjects, problem solve, and work with other students on their academic level" (Mr. S, personal communication, May 24, 2011).

Another disagreed, "If I had my choice between having gifted students and having learning support students in my class, I would probably choose the learning support" (Ms. W, personal communication, May 24, 2011).

The classroom teachers also need support. Jim Delisle, former teacher of gifted, has posted a letter of advice to new teachers where he lists these five reminders:

• Gifted education is often a hot political topic.
• Some of the top students in the school are not "gifted."
• As an advocate, teachers must believe in students when the students, and others, have doubts.
• Read about what has worked in the past—not just current fads.
• It is appropriate to be impressed by what these kids can do (adapted from Delisle, 2005).

He adds, "If you get the privilege to know gifted kids who continue to connect with you long after they leave your classroom, then you will truly know what it means to be a teacher" (Delisle, 2005, para. 9).

FROM PARENTS

The father of a nine-year-old who recently graduated from high school recalled that his profoundly gifted son was "speaking in sentences at seven months, reading and writing stories at age two, and doing multiplication by age two and division by age three" (Perrine, 2016, para. 1). Creating a board game to teach the periodic table at age seven, this nine-year-old watches TV, loves books, video games, and computers, and has ambitions to study astrophysics (Perrine, 2016). Although his dad calls him a "normal kid" (Perrine, 2016), students who are this profoundly gifted are found in less than 0.5 percent of the population (Wilderdom, 2005).

Most parents are not dealing with that level of giftedness, but still have issues and concerns. Peter DeWitt, advocate for gifted education, recently quoted the listing composed by Joshua Reynold, a former gifted student and current father of three. The article, "14 Things Gifted Students Want

Teachers to Know," comes from a parent perspective. His list (adapted below) reinforces many of the key points in previous chapters, but is worth repeating here:

1. Students want to learn new things. If they already know something, it is no longer fun and can even be distressing.
2. The repetition needed for most learners is not required for gifted students. Once might do it.
3. Gifted students—all students—should be encouraged to make connections to previous learning and to explore topics in depth.
4. Look for the twice-exceptional students and do not underestimate them.
5. Do not draw attention to gifted students. "Academic success isn't tolerated like success in sports. Grouping several [students] who are ahead to work together gives [them] a support group and doesn't make [them] as much of a target for bullies" (Reynold as quoted in DeWitt, 2016, item 5).
6. Understand that gifted students can be physically, mentally, or emotionally intense.
7. Place gifted students together in the same classroom. Dividing the best students among various classes may seem like being fair to the teachers and providing examples for slower students; it is not good policy (see *cluster grouping* in Chapters 4 and 5).
8. Be sensitive to asynchronous development. Placing an eight-year-old in middle school could present problems (see other methods of acceleration in Chapter 4).
9. Do not use gifted students as tutors for struggling students.
10. Gifted students need challenges. When schoolwork comes so easily, students may never learn how to study (see Chapter 6 for assessment strategies).
11. Always earning the top grades can lead to the need for perfectionism. In addition, the score rather than the learning becomes the goal.
12. Be aware that gifted students—especially elementary students—need to know that they are gifted in order to develop empathy for students who learn differently than they do. Their "normal" is all they know.
13. Know that these students can appear to be overconfident at all grade levels. Look for opportunities to encourage scholarly modesty but do so without public humiliation.
14. Gifted students at all levels are often reluctant to ask questions or to ask for help. Encouraging informal assessments and self-assessment strategies (as listed in Chapter 6) can promote understanding for teachers (adapted from DeWitt, 2016).

The parents of twice-exceptional students deal with many additional issues. A psychology professor from Iowa writes, "I truly believe we, as parents, educators, and psychologists, need to become better equipped to understand twice-exceptional students' individual differences. We need to set them up for success instead of letting them fall through the cracks" (Foley-Nicpon, 2015, p. 249).

A mother who has experienced the frustration of her son "falling through the cracks" wrote,

> My 7-year-old son ... is twice exceptional: profoundly gifted and learning disabled. As his mother, I often feel frustrated with the public's understanding of giftedness. Far too many people equate giftedness with achievement. They assume that gifted children have it easier, that they have an advantage over their peers. These folks see gifted education as elite and unnecessary. I have little doubt that many of these misperceptions stem from the label itself: gifted. The label conjures up images of beautifully wrapped presents with neatly tied bows, images that are a stark contrast to the reality of giftedness ... (Kessler, n.d., para. 2).

A dad shared the advice that the wise gifted coordinator, who knew his middle school son, disclosed, "Do NOT try to argue or reason with him. You will never win. The best policy is to simply be a broken record such as, 'You are not permitted to get a tattoo; you are not permitted to get a tattoo.' He will cleverly attempt to lure you into a reasoning defense. Never go there."

Another parent shared that her gifted son around age 10 was questioning logic of Santa Claus. Frustrated by her attempts to avoid the topic, he waited until she was in the bathroom. Standing outside the bathroom door, he demanded, "Confirm or deny? Confirm or deny?" Exasperated by his persistence, she admitted that she reluctantly and softly confirmed.

A mother of an intellectually gifted teen revealed, "... [Name] is a beauty to look at, but feels excessively socially out-of-the-loop ... She imitates the 'normal' kids' behaviors, because she cannot relate to anyone if she is just being herself. It's been a tough decade so far!"

STUDENTS SPEAK OUT

Gifted students faking it to act "normal" is not unique. A college student remembered his middle and high school experiences: "... by singling me out, my teachers guaranteed I would be bullied relentlessly throughout school and unable to make friends unless I hid my intelligence, and pretended to be part of the crowd. Which I learned to start doing around age 14 and missed out on a lot of opportunities in high school ..."

Another college student reflected on his twice-exceptional elementary experiences:

> I remember a day in second grade when the whole class was sitting in a circle taking turns reading a book. I quietly watched as each person took his turn. The number of students between the readers and myself slowly dwindled while my pulse rate quickened. Everyone read so fast! Finally, it was my turn. "OK," I told myself, "slowly sound out each word, and I'll do fine." Despite my best efforts, I still got stuck on the five-letter words that everyone else read with ease. The entire class started laughing; what an idiot I was; everyone could read this but me. I finished reading a few sentences in what seemed like three hours, but at least it was over. The torture had ended. But Wait! The circle was going around again!! (Strop & Goldman, 2002, para. 1).

Imagination and creativity are often evident in student comments. The nine-year-old high school graduate was asked if he could do anything in the world, what it would be. He responded that he would like to "visit another solar system ... the diamond planet." He then clarified for the adult interviewer, "... It is made of pure carbon—not pure diamond" (Perrine, 2016).

The importance of the homeroom teacher's attitude and environment are underscored by two middle school students. Jack, in eighth grade, "I liked the gifted program in third and fourth grade, but I think it's even better in middle school" (Personal communication, May 26, 2016). In middle school, as Jack explained, he participates in advanced classes in most subjects and likes that he works with students on his level.

He recalled how the gifted program worked in elementary grades (a pull-out program) and explained that he always felt like he was missing something when he left the room, and even though the gifted classroom was "fun," he would have just as gladly stayed in the typical classroom.

Tina (also eighth grade) preferred her time in the elementary gifted classroom. "I liked being with the other girls in Ms. S' classroom and working on projects with them" (Personal communication, May 26, 2016). Tina was referring to her two good friends, also gifted, but in a different homeroom. However, Tina did not want to be singled out from the rest of the girls in the regular classroom and often worried about being different. Her comments validated the need for cluster grouping (see Chapter 4) and awareness of gifted females as a special population (see Chapter 5).

While looking to the future, gifted students can be a tough audience for their teachers. When asked for opinions on what makes a good teacher, students' answers were classified under three headings:

- Intellectual ability.
- Personal/social traits.
- Pedagogical methods (Vialle & Tischler, 2009).

Under those headings, the student comments focused on five specific teacher characteristics: *knowledge, sense of humor, respect for students, patience,* and *organization* (Vialle & Tischler, 2009).

The letter in Box 8.1 is an example of how one gifted student reacted to her perception of a teacher who is less than qualified. Her letter addresses four of the characteristic areas as listed above. She questions the teacher's knowledge; mentions that he did not respect her work by cutting her off; refers to his lack of patience by interrupting her response; and suggests that he was not prepared for class.

Box 8.1

ALTHOUGH THE NAMES WERE CHANGED, THIS LETTER IS REPRINTED WITH PERMISSION FROM THE AUTHOR AND FROM HER PARENTS

Dr. _____ , [Superintendent of Schools]

My name is [Jane Doe], and I'm currently in seventh grade at _____ Middle School. As the school year has progressed, I've become increasingly concerned about my science teacher there, Mr. D. I spent a considerable part of the year assuming that I didn't understand the curriculum, but at this point I'm willing to say that I have doubts as to whether or not we even had a curriculum.

I met with [the building principal] a while back, and expressed a few of my concerns surrounding Mr. D. He explained that [our middle school] was in the process of creating a more defined science curriculum, but nothing has changed since.

Soon after my meeting with [the principal], Mr. D. began our ecosystems unit—if you can call it a unit—by showing his vacation photos from SeaWorld. I feel that this would be incomplete without mentioning his unusual penchant for personal—and often irrelevant—stories, photos, and videos. While I understand the value of media in class, and have been in many strongly media-based classes, Mr. D. seems to have difficulty using them to his advantage. For example, he briefly allowed his students to send him videos which, if deemed "relevant" (a term he uses loosely) would be shown in class. Although I don't want to put down my classmates, few of them are interested in finding truly good content, and many a minute has been wasted with a clip from *The Ellen Show* or *The Simpsons*. (Both, I may add, were real instances.)

As much as I appreciate Mr. D.'s attempts to tie his teaching into his students' daily lives, it's become clear that the majority of the media he uses in class is intended only to kill time, and are immensely frustrating to diligent students.

Mr. D. also teaches my math class, in the same two-hour block as science. Although I'm aware of complaints as far as math is concerned, I feel that our class has made progress over the year. However, math often spills into science, and regularly fills it

(continued)

completely. This, to me, feels like being cheated out of science class. I can't help but be a bit upset when Mr. D. tells us how proud he is that we've done almost double the planned work in math, when he is oblivious to the fact that we're rapidly falling behind in science.

One of my largest frustrations, however, is Mr. D.'s complete lack of preparation. He regularly asks us to be prepared for class and to transition quickly, but it would seem, from the perspective of one of his students, that he himself is rarely prepared. The majority of our larger projects—the ones that supposedly determine our grade—are things he comes up with while in the midst of talking abstractly in class. I find this extremely aggravating, to say the least.

Our most recent science project, for example, was a "work of art, expressing what we'd learned about ecosystems." Mr. D. had us sit quietly in class while he essentially developed his lesson plan. (He said that allowing us to contribute would help us learn, although it appeared a thinly veiled attempt at not having to work at home or during his plan time.) The premise of the project seemed to be to create some sort of work of art representing several key parts of an ecosystem, the most stressed of which was population. I spent a good three hours trying to research the "numerical data" he'd requested, only to come up with a government website saying that such a number could not be reached.

This frustrated me more than anything else. Had Mr. D. taken the time necessary to research his topic and prepare to teach it, he would have seen that he had assigned something that is widely regarded as unable to be determined. I finished the project to the best of my ability and went into school on Monday prepared to talk to him about the project.

When I began telling him what I'd found (essentially that population is not a reasonable number to determine), he was quick to cut me off and interrupt me. I tried to explain to him that government and environmental groups had routinely measured population inconsistently, but he insisted it was due to budget cuts. This was what he later told to the class, and it bothered me that—aside from being untrue—he hadn't so much as looked into it himself. I strongly feel that his seeming unwillingness to research or prepare and his inability to commit to a coherent course of study are seriously compromising science education at [the middle school].

I think that this has reached a point where it is putting the entire class noticeably behind in science. Although he is a passable math teacher, and I realize that the issue may lie partially in how the science curriculum is structured, Mr. D.'s lack of dedication is doing a disservice to all of his students. My goal in meeting with you is more to point out a consistent issue than to cause any problems, and I hope you understand that.

Thank you for your time.

Although the names have been omitted by request, the student who wrote that letter is currently in high school. She smiles as she relates that the summer after she wrote that letter, her parents were informed that she should skip eighth grade and move directly from grade seven to grade nine at the high school. Because it would be a new environment for all students, she and her parents agreed. She has been successful, made good friends, scores well in AP courses, and has not had a need to write any more letters to principals or to the superintendent. And as for the science/math teacher, he is currently teaching only math.

A study of gifted students produced the following statements. From a high school female: "Abilities a good teacher should have: a great knowledge; knows what he/she teaches; is friendly and understands us; the ability to explain clearly and precise[ly]; should come prepared for lessons" (Vialle & Tischler, 2009, p. 5).

From a middle-school male, "They have to be kind and understanding and let us learn at our own pace. They should enjoy teaching and know their subject well" (Vialle & Tischler, 2009, p. 5).

A high school student recently compared two teachers of AP Social Studies. Both of these male teachers were dedicated to having students pass the AP tests. One was described as approachable, flexible and personable; the other more aloof and demanding. The student revealed that the friendlier teacher's students passed the tests with a range of passing scores; the tougher teacher's students all earned the highest passing score. The student admitted that many students preferred the personable teacher for class and would take their chances with the AP scores (R.C., personal communication, June 25, 2016).

Students from elementary through high school agreed on the following teacher preferences. The teachers should:

- have interest in a wide variety of topics;
- have enthusiasm and passion for their subjects that is "contagious";
- present challenges—motivating;
- communicate the importance of topic;
- want to be in the classroom;
- vary teaching methods to be "entertaining";
- be organized;
- know how to control the class;
- be willing to admit mistakes or not knowing everything;
- be open to multiple viewpoints;
- provide timely and constructive feedback.

On the negative side, students recognized that unsuccessful teachers exhibited poor people skills, had an inability to simplify or explain the subject, and became impatient when students did not understand (Vialle & Tischler, 2009). As a high school student wrote, "It's no good having someone who knows all the intricacies of a subject but then they can't teach us and get fed up when we don't understand" (Vialle & Tischler, 2009, p. 7).

Although providing opportunities for risk-taking and failing was not on the student list, a group of high school students recalled a time in middle school when they experienced true failure. "We entered a group science competition. We thought we would rock it. Not only did we finish last, our score was embarrassingly low. This 'epic failure' was an eye-opener" (R.C. and T.W., personal communication, July 25, 2016).

Another "eye-opener" is a resource book for teachers of twice-exceptional students that was developed by the Colorado Department of Education (2012). Quotes from students identified as twice-exceptional reveal their being "frustrated," feeling "stupid," worried about "disease, terrorism, and war," or planning "to quit school ..." A student identified as ADHD and gifted sadly summed it up with, "I'm just stupid ... I forget everything and never finish anything!" (Colorado Department of Education, 2012, pp. 53–56).

GIFTED ADULTS REMEMBER

Adults recalling their experiences with gifted education add to the voices. "I often thought that I was really stupid because I couldn't understand why teachers taught things that I thought were obvious. I thought the other children were smarter because they saw complexities that I now know never existed. I had a hard time understanding other children. It never occurred to me that I felt different because I was ahead of them intellectually" (Ruf, 2000, para. 7).

An attorney who admits that he almost dropped out of high school due to boredom and social isolation recalled, "I took a swing at the teacher in second grade because she was making fun of my vocabulary ... I would get bad grades because I never did my homework. I could have ended up a really well-read homeless person" (As cited in Kamenetz, 2015, para. 5).

Heidi Molbak, Founder and President of Seed Started Educational Counseling for Gifted and Twice-Exceptional Students concludes that "... widely-reported research shows that being a 'smart' girl is not a ticket to a happy life ..." (as cited in Kerr & McKay, 2014, flyleaf).

The authors of *What Science Tells Us about Raising Successful Children* warn, "We're training kids to do what computers do, which is spit back facts. And computers are always going to be better than human beings at that. But what they're not going to be better at is being social, navigating relationships, being citizens in a community. So we need to change the whole definition of what success in school, and out of school, means" (Roberta Michnick Golinkoff and Kathy Hirsh-Pasek as cited in Kamenetz, 2016, para. 9).

A current college professor of education who has experienced most of the roles in this chapter—gifted student, parent of gifted children, teacher of gifted students, and researcher of gifted theories—summed it up by saying, "Although we still have miles to go, we need to celebrate the vast growth in gifted education throughout the past twenty years. Recognizing the variety of needs of gifted students is the first step that gives us direction to prepare successful contributing members of society. And that should always be our goal" (Dr. A.M., professor of education, personal communication, June 2016).

SUMMARY

Awareness of meeting the complex needs of gifted student is on the upswing. Social media with blogs, online articles, and sharing comments and experiences add to the community conscience and concern about special populations of gifted students. This chapter provided a sampling of comments and experiences from a variety of stakeholders in gifted education.

FOOD FOR THOUGHT

- Choose one of the voices "heard" in this chapter and reflect on the one that speaks to you. What personal connections can you make to those words?

Chapter Nine

Resources

"With so much information now online, it is exceptionally easy to simply dive in and drown."

Alfred Glossbrenner

Finding information and resources for gifted education is not difficult. Type "Gifted Education Resources" into a search engine and over a million links will pop up. However, finding the worthwhile resources among those million links can be overwhelming. This chapter describes some of the most popular sites and documents on the topic that are appropriate for parents and teachers.

FREE HANDBOOKS AND GUIDES

Teachers love free—who doesn't? An excellent free resource is *The Department of Defense Education Activity Program Guide for Gifted Education.* An easy download, it is available as PDF file. In addition to a wealth of background information, it also has 20 forms and templates for checklists, parent letters, assessment rubrics, and rating scales for students in grades K-12 for teachers and parents to complete. Simply type the guide's title into a search engine or use this URL: http://www.dodea.edu/Curriculum/ giftedEduc/upload/ge_programGuide_full.pdf

Especially useful, the Department of Defense Education Activity (DoDEA) Guide also gives advice for using higher order questions with examples. Their recommendations include the following:

GUIDELINES FOR HIGHER ORDER QUESTIONING

- Avoid questions with "yes" or "no" or any other one-word answer.
- Follow-up answers with higher order questions.
- Ask only one question at a time.
- Vary the questioning techniques.
- Have students paraphrase what they have heard and write their own questions.
- Encourage students to answer each other, not only the teacher.

They also provide sample questions such as:

- Clarification
    o Could you give me an example?
    o Could you put that another way?
    o What do you think is the main issue?
    o Would you summarize in your own words?
- Assumptions
    o What are you assuming?
    o Is it always the case?
    o Why would someone make this assumption?
- Reasons and Evidence
    o Why do you think that is true?
    o What evidence do you have for that?
    o How could we find out whether that is true?
- Viewpoints or Perspectives
    o Why have you chosen this perspective?
    o How would other groups/types of people respond? Why?
    o What would someone who disagrees say?
    o What is an alternative?
- Implications and Consequences
    o What would happen as a result? Why?
    o What is an alternative?
    o If this is the case, what must also be true? (adapted from Department of Defense Education Activity, 2006, pp. 92–93).

Montgomery County School District in Maryland provides a free *Guidebook for Twice Exceptional Students* that contains excellent tables of comparisons of student traits. Use its title or this URL to access it: http://www.wrightslaw.com/info/2e.guidebook.pdf

For examples of specific situations, the Colorado Department of Education also provides a handbook complete with case studies and follow-ups on teaching 2e students. Especially useful are tables of "Distinguishing Characteristics of Gifted Students." These tables detail how traits many appear when influenced by *culture, disability*, or *socio-economic factors*. The handbook can be accessed by title: *Twice-Exceptional Students: Gifted Students with Disabilities, Level 1: An Introductory Resource Book* or by using the following URL http://www.cde.state. co.us/sites/default/files/documents/gt/download/pdf/level_1_resource_ handbook_4th_ed_10-2-12.pdf

GOVERNMENT RESOURCES

Because the federal government is involved in gifted education, the two Congressional websites provide current links to lawmakers and to legislation:

- House of Representatives http://www.house.gov/
- Senate http://www.senate.gov/index.htm

State departments of education are also an excellent governmental source. The homepage of the National Society for the Gifted and Talented provides alphabetical links for each state department of education as well as independent state-based organizations that are advocates for gifted education within that state:

- State Groups from all 50 states (government and independent) http://www. nsgt.org/state-organizations/

The state departments of gifted education are taxpayer funded and are under the umbrella of state departments of education. In contrast, membership fees usually fund the independent groups in each state. In addition to providing support for local programs and for parents, the independent state groups often provide lobbyists, organize workshops or conferences, and provide updated information.

NATIONAL ORGANIZATIONS

Nationwide organizations are usually membership-based. They provide research and advocacy recommendations. Twelve national groups are listed on the National Society for the Gifted and Talented site: http://www.nsgt.org/ national-organizations/

Other well-known national groups with their links are as follows:

- Hoagies' Gifted Education Page http://www.hoagiesgifted.org/
- National Association for Gifted Children Homepage: http://www.nagc.org/
- National Society for the Gifted and Talented http://www.nsgt.org/
- Duke University Talent Identification Program http://tip.duke.edu/
- Hunter College Center for Gifted Education http://www.hunter.cuny.edu/
  gt-center/

LOCAL SCHOOL DISTRICTS AND SUMMER PROGRAMS

While searching for information on gifted students, it is wise to review the policies of area public and private schools. Checking the websites of regional school districts can provide insights into local gifted education information.

Local districts often have summer programs listed. Camps sponsored by school districts such as "Camp Einstein" in Norfolk, VA, can provide ideas for developing local summer programs; State Governor's Summer Schools are available in many of the states and are often tuition free.

TEACHER PREPARATION PROGRAM STANDARDS

The National Association for Gifted Children (NAGC) and the Council for Exceptional Children (CEC) developed the following ten research-based standards for teacher preparation programs in gifted education. These programs must include the following:

- Standard 1: Foundations (theories, principles, laws, and policies)
- Standard 2: Development and Characteristics of Learners (differences, similarities, families, communities)
- Standard 3: Individual Learning Differences (language, culture, family background and special populations)
- Standard 4: Instructional Strategies (critical and creative thinking, problem solving and performance skills)
- Standard 5: Learning Environments and Social Interaction (safe environments that respect diversity)
- Standard 6: Language and Communication (oral, written, ELL, assistive technology)
- Standard 7: Instructional Planning (long-range plans and short-term goals anchored in both general and special curricula; differentiated instructional strategies)

- Standard 8: Assessment (identification, legal policies and ethical principles of measurement and assessment related to referral, eligibility, program planning, instruction and placement)
- Standard 9: Professional and Ethical Practice (reflective practitioners; lifelong learners)
- Standard 10: Collaboration (collaboration with families, other educators and related service providers; advocate for individuals with gifts and talents across settings and diverse learning experiences). (Adapted from Teach.com, 2016)

YOUTUBE VIDEOS

Another resource for teacher preparation or for professional development programs is the catalog of videos on gifted education as posted on YouTube. Although there are many excellent clips posted, the brief clips by Dr. Dan Peters of Summit Center are outstanding and relatively short. For a longer (sixty minutes) thorough view, a light-hearted presentation by Dr. Jim Delisle for parents is also YouTube available.

FORMS AND TEMPLATES

In addition to the sample templates provided by *The Department of Defense Education Activity Program Guide for Gifted Education* for checklists, letters and rating scales, there are varieties of models available that are specific to compacting the curriculum or creating learning contracts.

Compacting the Curriculum Forms

A range of outlines are available to simplify compacting the curriculum. Most forms include the following four areas:

- *Basic Information.* The top section is for demographics required by the district or school. This usually includes the student name, teachers, parents, school, grade, a place for conference date(s), and persons participating.

After the demographic section, the following three sections are to be completed:

- *Name It Section.* This section identifies the student's areas of strength with a listing of the curriculum area(s) to be considered for compacting. The objectives or standards may be listed here.

- *Prove It Section.* The second section documents or describes how the teacher determined the student knew the material. This may include test scores, observation data, behavior checklists, rubrics, or past records.
- *Change It Section.* This section describes the alternative work, acceleration plan, or enrichment activities that will be assessed to determine competency. This may include independent study, advanced honors courses, college courses, small group investigations, projects, or presentations. (Adapted from Giger, 2007; Coil, 2008; Reis & Renzulli, n.d; Winebrenner, 2012).

Learning Contract Forms

With signatures of participants, the compactor forms can also serve as a contract for learning. However, educators have used student contracts specific for behavior and for learning for many years. A sample used at the college level for independent study includes sections for the following:

- Objectives (What am I going to learn?)
- Strategies and Resources (How am I going to learn it?)
- Time Frame (When will I finish?)
- Evidence (How will I know that I have learned it?)
- Verification/Evaluation (How will I prove that I have learned it?

The above format would also be appropriate for gifted students from middle through high school. Learning contracts used at the elementary level include the following:

- Statement of purpose;
- Student actions;
- Teacher action;
- Signatures of student, teacher, and parents.

ARTICLES FOR PARENTS AND TEACHERS

Dr. Sylvia Rimm, a nationally known psychologist, is the director of Family Achievement Clinic in Cleveland and a clinical professor at Case Western Reserve School of Medicine. In addition to counseling on a variety of developmental issues, Dr. Rimm also guides gifted children and their families. She has a long list of worthwhile informational articles available at http://www.sylviarimm.com/parentingarticles.html An interesting component of Dr. Rimm's site is the area to submit a family or teaching question where she encourages inquiries from parents, grandparents, teachers, and young people.

THE LIGHTER SIDE OF GIFTED EDUCATION

Although gifted education is serious business, there always remains a humorous perspective. As one mother revealed, "I tried to prepare my seven-year-old son for being pulled out of class by the school psychologist to be tested for the gifted program. I gave the usual, you-are-not-in-trouble and don't-worry-about-what-she-asks speech. When he returned home, he said it was fine but then demanded, 'Why didn't you tell me she had a moustache?'"

The Hoagies' Gifted Education Page has a file of amusing narratives in its "You Know You're the Parent of a Gifted Child When ..." The section has a long list of humorous comments and anecdotes from these admittedly "quirky kids." Simply go to http://www.hoagiesgifted.org/parent_of.htm where the page is divided into *Younger, Older*, and *Even When* sections. In a similar vein, the Exquisite Minds website has a gifted humor archive of articles by Stacia Garland. Go to http://www.exquisite minds.com/category/humor/ for these essays.

Cathy Greene on the Right Side of the Curve website lists "10 Lessons from Benjamin Franklin That Might Help Advocates of Gifted Learners." Greene cleverly lists ten Franklin quotes and interprets them in the light of gifted education advocacy. Find them at http://www.rightsideofthecurve.com/articles/articles/advocacy/10-lessons-from-benjamin-franklin-that-might-help-advocates-of-gifted-learners

Parents of gifted children are also clever and creative. There are several links to Mary Beth Northrup's clever poem "If Dr. Seuss Had a Gifted Child." Written in 1998 as an eight-stanza Seuss-style rhyming dialog between parent and teacher, the poem is still applicable today. Because the work is copyrighted and the author was not available to grant permission to reprint, only the first two lines are printed here. However, the entire poem is offered at http://www.ri.net/gifted_talented/parents.html

"Dear Mom-I-am, dear Mom-I-am, we have a problem, Mom-I-am.
Your son won't do what he must do. He drives me crazy, yes it's true!"
(Northrup, 1998, para. 1)

SUMMARY

This chapter provided information and links to resources for gifted education from government links to free documents, forms, and templates. Also included were links to sites for teachers and parents that focus on humor in gifted education.

At the time of publication, all of the website addresses (URLs) were checked for availability and accuracy. However, some sites on the web have a short "shelf-life" and disappear without warning. Lost sites often can be relocated by typing in the name of the site into a search engine such as Google or Yahoo.

Another resource for lost sites is to use the "Way Back Machine" website at http://www.archive.org/index.php to locate the change of address locations. At this site, you simply type in the old URL and it takes you to the new address if available.

FOOD FOR THOUGHT

- Research and analyze templates used for compacting the curriculum and learning contracts. Which ones appeal to you; which ones do not? What you would add or delete?
- Find Internet sites and mobile apps appropriate for students identified as gifted to use in the classroom as enrichment. Keep in mind Passow's (1988) three-question test for differentiation as a quick way to validate enrichment activities (see Chapter 4).

Epilogue

Answering the Question

GIFTED OR JUST PLAIN SMART?

If you have read this entire book, you realize that it presented research, supporting data, and advice from experts. Even with the help of lists of characteristics (Table 3.1), discriminating between gifted or just plain smart continues to be a challenge for all educators.

Usually there are two large distinct groups of students identified as gifted. In one large group are the students who know how to "do school." These are the ones who get the As, complete all the assignments, score highest on standardized tests. They jump through every teacher hoop and seldom make waves. These students are incredibly smart; they will be successful in their chosen careers. They meet the first column of the Smart, Gifted, Creative Chart in Table 3.1. They *are* smart (and there is nothing *plain* about them).

The second group are the "quirky" ones who are usually "truly gifted" in that they see the world through different lenses than most of us. They definitely rock the boat and can even be a rock star. Look at the second column of Table 3.1 for descriptors of truly gifted.

And since "creative" was also tossed into the mix, we cannot ignore those who are described by characteristics in the third column of that listing. These dreamers of wild ideas with many talents are seldom overlooked.

The fourth category—not on that chart—would be the geniuses or "profoundly gifted." As discussed in Chapter 8, these students are calculated to be in the top 0.4 percent of the population (Wilderdom, 2005). Most of us will not have a student who finishes high school by age 9. Because very few children do higher level math at age 2 or speak in sentences at six months, identifying that precocious group is often easy.

But what is *not* easy is meeting needs. As one mom put it, "Even just plain smart ones can be tough." Here is the bottom line—the labels really do not matter. What does matter is that these children are learning *new material* during their school day. Children who are labeled as smart, gifted, profoundly gifted, or creative all deserve the same opportunity to learn as do all our children with a wide range of learning capabilities. And, yes, it is one more task for teachers to add to their ever-growing list of responsibilities.

The good news is that with an increasing awareness of this need, help is available. Chapter 9 lists many resources, textbook publishers continue to add "enrichment activities" to their teacher manuals, and universities and state departments of education are beginning to add gifted education to their lists of specialties. So, whether a child is gifted, just plain smart, or creative, teaching or parenting the ninety-ninth percentile can be a wild ride. Hang on and smile!

References

ASCD (2016). Multiple measures of assessment. *ASCD SmartBrief*. Retrieved: www. ascd.com

Associated Press (2016). Clinton has reinvented herself more than once. *Tribune Review, Westmoreland Edition*. 128(177), A4.

Assouline, S., Colangelo, N., VanTassel-Baska, J., & Lupkowski-Shoplik, A. (Eds.) (2015). *A nation empowered: Evidence trumps the excuses holding back America's brightest students*. Acceleration Institute, Belin-Blank Center, University of Iowa. Retrieved: http://www.accelerationinstitute.org/Nation_Empowered/Default.aspx

Barbaro, R.W. (n.d.). Psyography: Leta Stetter Hollingworth. Retrieved: http:// faculty.frostburg.edu/mbradley/psyography/letastetterhollingworth.html

Bauer, S., Benkstein, P., Pittel, A., & Koury, G. (n.d.). Gifted students: Recommendations for teachers. Retrieved: http://www.education.udel.edu/wpcontent/uploads/2013/ 01/GiftedStudents.pdf

Berman, K.M., Schultz, R.A., & Weber, C.L. (2012). A lack of awareness and emphasis in preservice teacher training: Preconceived beliefs about the gifted and talented. *Gifted Child Today*. 35(1), 19–26. Retrieved: http://dx.doi.org/10.1177/1076217511428307

Blad, E. (2016). Disparities continue to plague US schools, federal data show. *Education Week*. Retrieved: http://www.edweek.org/ew/articles/2016/06/07/disparities-continue-to-plague-us-schools-federal.html?tkn=TNOF4NpmV8mxxfmukxLeiFI3yP9EIfLu R2hf&intc=es

Bracamonte, M. (2010). Twice-exceptional students: Who are they and what do they need? Retrieved: http://www.2enewsletter.com/article_2e_what_are_they.html

Brain Balance Achievement Centers (2016). Identifying twice-exceptional children. Retrieved: http://www.brainbalancecenters.com/blog/2015/02/ identifying-twice-exceptional-children/

Brody, L.E., & Mills, C.J. (2004). Linking assessment and diagnosis to intervention for gifted students with learning disabilities. In T. Newman, & R J. Sternberg (Eds.), *Students with both gifts and learning disabilities*. New York: Kluwer Academic Publishers.

Brown, E. (2016). New federal civil rights data show persistent racial gaps in discipline, access to advanced coursework. *Washington Post*. Retrieved: https://www.washingtonpost.com/local/education/new-federal-civil-rights-data-show-persistent-racial-gaps-in-discipline-access-to-advanced-coursework/2016/06/06/e95a4386-2bf2-11e6-9b37-42985f6a265c_story.html?tid=a_inl

Brown, E.F. (2015). Serving gifted students in general ed classrooms. Retrieved: http://www.edutopia.org/blog/gifted-students-general-ed-classrooms-elissa-brown

Caldwell, D.W. (2012). Educating gifted students in the regular classroom: Efficacy, attitudes, and differentiation of instruction. Retrieved: http://digitalcommons.georgiasouthern.edu/cgi/viewcontent.cgi?article=1826&context=etd

Callahan, C.M. (2010). Lessons learned from evaluation programs for the gifted. Retrieved: http://www.k12.wa.us/HighlyCapable/Workgroup/pubdocs/PresentationbyCallahan9-16-10.pdf

Callard-Szulgit, R. (2008). *Twice-exceptional kids*. Landham, MD: Rowman & Littlefield Education.

Carolyn, K. (2016). Twice exceptional = exceptional squared! Hoagies' Gifted Education Page. Retrieved: http://www.hoagiesgifted.org/2e_exceptional.htm

Cherry, K. (2015a). Genius IQ score? Retrieved: http://psychology.about.com/od/psychologicaltesting/f/genius-iq-score.htm

Cherry, K. (2015b). Theories of intelligence. Retrieved: http://psychology.about.com/od/cognitivepsychology/p/intelligence.htm

Coil, C. (2008). Keys to successful district wide differentiation: Training, time, practice, and sharing. *E-Zine*. 2, 3. Retrieved: http://www.carolyncoil.com/ezine21.htm

Coil, C. (2012). My view: Ten myths about gifted students and programs for gifted. Retrieved: http://schoolsofthought.blogs.cnn.com/2012/11/14/ten-myths-about-gifted-students-and-programs-for-gifted/

Colangelo, N., Assouline, S.G., & Gross, M.U.M. (Eds.) (2004). *A nation deceived: How schools hold back America's brightest students*. The Templeton National Report on Acceleration, Vol. 1. Retrieved: http://www2.education.uiowa.edu/belinblank/pdfs/ND_v1.pdf

Colorado Department of Education (2012). *Twice-exceptional students: Gifted students with disabilities. An introductory resource book*. Retrieved: http://www.cde.state.co.us/sites/default/files/documents/gt/download/pdf/level_1_resource_handbook_4th_ed_10-2-12.pdf

Colucci, A. (2015). Gifted ed. students are more than just really smart kids. *Education Week Teacher*. Retrieved: http://www.edweek.org/tm/articles/2015/11/24/understanding-giftedstudents.html?tkn=XZNDi2NpLJsJjfFR2RGw6rClMLDhpWlKVzu6&intc=es&print=1

Comallie-Caplan, L. (2013). Raising gifted girls into gifted women. Retrieved: http://www.negifted.org/NAG/Spring_Conference_files/Gifted%20Girls%20to%20Gifted%20Women%20-%20handouts.pdf

Conrad, L. (2016). Every Student Succeeds Act and gifted education. Retrieved: https://globalgtchatpoweredbytagt.wordpress.com/2016/01/25/every-student-succeeds-act-and-gifted-education/

Council for Exceptional Children (CEC) (2013). Issue brief. Retrieved: https://www.cec.sped.org/~/media/Files/Policy/Issue%20Brief%20Special%20Gifted%20Funding%20July%202013.pdf

Cox, J. (n.d.). Teaching strategies to aid your gifted students. Retrieved: http://www.teachhub.com/teaching-strategies-aid-your-gifted-students

Davidson Institute (2016a). Gifted education state policies. Retrieved: http://www.davidsongifted.org/db/StatePolicy.aspx

Davidson Institute (2016b). Tips for teachers: Successful strategies for teaching gifted learners. Retrieved: http://www.davidsongifted.org/db/Articles_id_10075.aspx

Delisle, J.R. (2005). A message to new teachers of gifted children. *Gifted Child Today*. 28(1), 22–23.

Department of Defense Education Activity (2006). *Gifted education program guide.* Retrieved: http://www.dodea.edu/Curriculum/giftedEduc/upload/ge_programGuide_full.pdf

DeWitt, P. (2016). 14 things gifted students want teachers to know. *Finding Common Ground.* Retrieved: https://rochestersage.org/2016/07/06/14-things-gifted-students-want-teachers-to-know/

Digest of Gifted Research (2015). Giftedness and masculinity: Balancing expectations. Retrieved: https://tip.duke.edu/node/1657

Duke Talent Identification Program. (2006). Being a gifted boy: What we have learned. *Digest of Gifted Research.* Retrieved: https://tip.duke.edu/node/651

Duke Talent Identification Program (2015a). Gifted girls and messages about success. *Digest of Gifted Research.* Retrieved: https://tip.duke.edu/node/1658

Duke Talent Identification Program (2015b). Instructional strategies. Retrieved: https://tip.duke.edu/node/347

Educational Testing (2014). 10 years of advanced placement exam data. Retrieved: https://www.collegeboard.org/releases/2014/class-2013-advanced-placement-results-announced

Estes, S.E. (n.d.). Education law: The Jacob J. Javits Gifted and Talented Students Education Act. Retrieved: http://usedulaw.com/352-jacob-k-javits-gifted-and-talented-students-education-act.html

Fliess, S.D. (2009). Twice-exceptional children. Retrieved: http://www.education.com/magazine/article/Ed_Twice_Exceptional/

Foley-Nicpon, M. (2015). Voices from the field: The higher education community. *Gifted Child Today.* 38(4), 249–251.

Freishtat, S. (2016). District 308 overhauling gifted education program. *Chicago Tribune Aurora Beacon News.* Retrieved: http://www.chicagotribune.com/suburbs/aurora-beacon-news/news/ct-abn-district-308-gifted-ed-st-0609-20160608-story.html

Gagné, F. (2008). Building gifts into talents: Brief overview of the DMGT. Retrieved: http://nswagtc.org.au/images/stories/infocentre/dmgt_2.0_en_overview.pdf

Giger, M. (2007). Curriculum compacting. Retrieved: http://www.gigers.com/matthias/gifted/sem-compacting.html

Ginott, H. (1975). *Teacher and child.* New York: Avon.

Goodkin, S., & Gold, D.G. (2007). The gifted children left behind. *Washington Post.* Retrieved: http://www.washingtonpost.com/wp-dyn/content/article/2007/08/26/AR2007082600909.html?referrer=emailarticle

Haggarty, K. (2013). Gifted and talented learners. Retrieved: https://prezi.com/qlh-6fa45ostd/gifted-and-talented-learners/

Hawaii Public Schools (n.d.). General learner outcomes. GLO 3 complex thinker. Retrieved: http://doe.k12.hi.us/curriculum/GLO_rubric_grade1-6.htm

Hawking, S. (n.d.). BrainyQuote.com. Retrieved: http://www.brainyquote.com/quotes/quotes/s/stephenhaw378304.html

Hearne, J., & Maurer, B. (2000). Gifted education: A primer. John Hopkins School of Education Retrieved: http://education.jhu.edu/PD/newhorizons/Exceptional%20Learners/Gifted%20Learners/Articles%20-%20Gifted%20Learners/gifted_education_a_primer.htm

Heath, W.J. (1997). What are the most effective characteristics of teachers of the gifted? *Eric Document*. 411, 665.

Hoagies' Gifted Education Page (2016). Gender issues. Retrieved: http://www.hoagiesgifted.org/gender.htm

International Baccalaureate (n.d.). United States. Retrieved: http://www.ibo.org/country/US/

Islas, M.R. (2016). Chief state schools officers' memo. Requirements in Every Student Succeeds Act about gifted learners. Retrieved: http://www.nagc.org/uploadedFiles/Information_and_Resources/NCATE_standards/NAGC-%20CEC%20CAEP%20standards%20(2013%20final).pdf

Johnsen, S.K. (2009). Best practices for identifying gifted. *Principal*. Retrieved: https://www.naesp.org/resources/2/Principal/2009/M-J_p08.pdf

Kamenetz, A. (2015). Who are the "gifted and talented" and what do they need? Retrieved: http://www.npr.org/sections/ed/2015/09/28/443193523/who-are-the-gifted-and-talented-and-what-do-they-need

Kamenetz, A. (2016). How to raise brilliant children, according to science. Retrieved: http://www.npr.org/sections/ed/2016/07/05/481582529/how-to-raise-brilliant-children-according-to-science?utm_source=npr_newsletter&utm_medium=email&utm_content=20160710&utm_campaign=bestofnpr&utm_term=nprnews

Kerr, B.A., & McKay, R. (2014). *Smart girls in the 21st Century: Understanding talented girls and women*. Tuscon, AZ: Great Potential Press.

Kerr, B.A., Vuyk, A., & Rea, C. (2012). Gendered practices in the education of gifted girls and boys. *Psychology in the Schools*. 49, 647–655.

Kessler, C. (n.d.). Raising lifelong learners. Retrieved: http://www.raisinglifelonglearners.com/asynchronous-development/

Kingore, B. (2004). High achiever, gifted learner, creative learner. *Understanding Our Gifted*. Retrieved: http://www.bertiekingore.com/high-gt-create.htm

Kotter, E F. (2008). Giftedness: Too smart to go to school? Unpublished manuscript: Sunbridge, NY.

Langille, J. (2003). Gifted girls and gender issues. *ABC Newsmagazine*. Retrieved: http://janelangille.com/wp-content/uploads/2011/03/WebOct2003.pdf

Mills, C.J. (2003). Characteristics of effective teachers of gifted students: Teacher background and personality styles of students. *Gifted Child Quarterly*. 47(4), 272–281.

Martinson, R.A. (1975). *The identification of the gifted and talented*. Reston, VA: The Council for Exceptional Children.

McClellan, E. (1985). Defining giftedness. ERIC ID ED262519. Retrieved: http://www.ericdigests.org/pre-923/defining.htm

MENSA (2015). IQ scale. Retrieved: https://www.iqtestforfree.net/iq-scale.html

Moran, K. (2016). Spotting giftedness in her students becomes a lesson in inclusion for this teacher. Retrieved: http://www.pri.org/stories/2016-06-06/spotting-giftedness-her-students-becomes-lesson-inclusion-teacher

Morehead, J. (2012). Stanford University's Carol Dweck on the growth mindset and education. Retrieved: https://onedublin.org/2012/06/19/stanford-universitys-carol-dweck-on-the-growth-mindset-and-education/

Morelock, M.J. (1992). Giftedness: The view from within. Retrieved: http://www.davidsongifted.org/db/Articles_id_10172.aspx

Moursund, D.G. (2005). *Increasing your expertise as a problem solver: Some roles of computers*. Eugene, OR: ISTE.

National Association for Gifted Children (NAGC) (n.d.a.). A brief history of gifted and talented education. Retrieved: http://www.nagc.org/resources-publications/resources/gifted-education-us/brief-history-gifted-and-talented-education

National Association for Gifted Children (NAGC) (n.d.b.). Myths about gifted students. Retrieved: https://www.nagc.org/resources-publications/resources/myths-about-gifted-students

National Association for Gifted Children (NAGC) (n.d.c.). Identifying gifted children from diverse populations. Retrieved: https://www.nagc.org/resources-publications/resources/timely-topics/ensuring-diverse-learner-participation-gifted-0

National Association for Gifted Children (NAGC) (n.d.d.). National standards in gifted and talented education. Retrieved: https://www.nagc.org/resources-publications/resources/national-standards-gifted-and-talented-education

National Association for Gifted Children (NAGC). (2014) University services, coursework, & degree programs in gifted and talented education. Retrieved: http://www.nagc.org/sites/default/files/Gifted-by-State/Coursework%20and%20Degree%20Programs%20FINAL%20DOCUMENT_0.pdf

National Association for Gifted Children (NAGC) (2015). Knowledge and skill standards in gifted education for all teachers. Retrieved: https://www.nagc.org/resources-publications/resources/national-standards-gifted-and-talented-education/knowledge-and

National Association for Gifted Children & the Council of State Directors of Programs for the Gifted (2015). State of the states in gifted education policy and practice data http://www.nagc.org/sites/default/files/key%20reports/2014-2015%20State%20of%20the%20States%20summary.pdf

NEA (2006). *The twice-exceptional dilemma*. Retrieved: http://www.nea.org/assets/docs/twiceexceptional.pdf

Northrup, M.B. (1998). If Dr. Seuss had a gifted child. Parents Resources. The Rhode Island State Advisory Committee on Gifted and Talented Education. Retrieved: http://www.ri.net/gifted_talented/parents.html

Olson, P. (n.d.). What is gifted education? History, models, & issues. Retrieved: http://study.com/academy/lesson/what-is-gifted-education-history-models-issues.html

Olszewski-Kubilius, P., Subotnik, R., & Worrell, F. (2012). Where are the gifted minorities? *Scientific American*. Retrieved: http://www.davidsongifted.org/db/Articles_id_10759.aspx

Olszewski-Kubilius, P., & Thomson, D. (2013). Gifted education programs and procedures. In I.B. Weiner, W.M. Reynolds, & G.E. Miller (Eds.), *Handbook of psychology, educational psychology (Volume 7)*. (pp. 389–407). Hoboken, NJ: Wiley and Sons.

Oregon Technology in Education Council (2007). Theories of intelligence. Retrieved: http://otec.uoregon.edu/intelligence.htm

Quinlan, A.M. (2012). *A complete guide to rubrics: Assessment made easy for teachers of k-college*. 2nd ed. Landham, MD: Rowman & Littlefield Education.

Passow, A.H. (1988). The educating and schooling of the community artisans in science. In P.F. Brandwein, & A.H. Passow (Eds.), *Gifted young in science: Potential through performance*. (pp. 27–38). Washington, DC: National Teachers Association.

Perin, M. (n.d.) Fair and equal—what's the difference? Retrieved: http://edhelper.com/ReadingComprehension_54_2585.html

Perrine, S. (2016). Pint-sized genius graduated Penn-Trafford High School at 9, but is still a normal kid. WTAE Channel 4. Retrieved: http://www.wtae.com/news/pintsized-genius-graduates-penntrafford-high-school-at-9-but-is-still-a-normal-kid/40107718

Peters, S.J., Kaufman, S.B., Matthews, M.S, McBee, M.T., & McCoach, D.B. (2014). Gifted ed. is crucial, but the label isn't. *Ed Week*. 33(28), 34–40.

Purcell, J.H., & Eckert, R.D. (Eds.) (n.d.). *Designing services and programs for high ability learners: A guidebook for gifted education*. Thousand Oaks, CA: Sage. Retrieved: http://www.k12.wa.us/HighlyCapable/Workgroup/pubdocs/designing-servicesandprograms15.pdf

Ramsey, I. (1990). Who should teach the gifted? *The Clearing House*. 63(8), 351–354. Retrieved: https://www.jstor.org/stable/30188521?seq=1#page_scan_tab_contents

Reis, S. (2002). Social and emotional issues faced by gifted girls in elementary and secondary schools. *SENG Newsletter*. 2(3), 1–5. Retrieved: http://sengifted.org/archives/articles/social-and-emotional-issues-faced-by-gifted-girls-in-elementary-and-secondary-school

Reis, S.M., & Renzulli J.S. (1984). Key features of successful programs for the gifted and talented. *Education Leadership, ASCD*. 28–34. Retrieved: http://www.ascd.org/ASCD/pdf/journals/ed_lead/el_198404_reis.pdf

Reis, S.M., & Renzulli J.S. (n.d.). Curriculum compacting: A systematic procedure for modifying the curriculum for above average ability students. Retrieved: http://gifted.uconn.edu/schoolwide-enrichment-model/curriculum_compacting/

Renzulli, J.S. (1978). What makes giftedness? *Phi Delta Kappan*. 60, 180–184.

Renzulli, J.S. (2005). The three-ring conception of giftedness: A developmental model for promoting creative productivity. In R.J. Sternberg, & J.E. Davidson (Eds.), *Conceptions of giftedness* (pp. 246–279). New York, NY: Cambridge University Press.

Rimm, P.B. (n.d.) Goodread quotes. Retrieved: http://www.goodreads.com/quotes/516953-the-surest-path-to-positive-self-esteem-is-to-succeed-at

Rockingham County Schools (2013). Dispelling myths, serving students. Retrieved: http://www.rock.k12.nc.us/Page/5084

Robinson, G. (2012). Gifted—or just privileged? Retrieved: http://www.greatschools.org/gk/articles/gifted-education-and-program-controversy/

Ruf, D.L. (2000). Social & emotional issues: What gifted adults say about their childhoods. Retrieved: http://www.educationaloptions.com/resources/resources_gifted_adults.php

Silverman, L.K. (2007). Asynchrony: A new definition of giftedness. *Digest of Gifted Research*. Retrieved: https://tip.duke.edu/node/839

Smutny, J.F. (2000). Teaching young gifted children in the regular classroom. The ERIC Clearinghouse on Disabilities and Gifted Education (ERIC EC). Digest #E595. Retrieved: http://www.hoagiesgifted.org/eric/e595.html

Sousa, D.A. (2009). *How the gifted brain learns*. 2nd ed. Thousand Oaks, CA: Corwin

Sternberg, R.J. (1985). *Beyond IQ: A triarchic theory of human intelligence*. New York, NY: Cambridge University Press.

Sternberg, R.J. (1997). A triarchic view of giftedness: Theory and practice. In N. Coleangelo, & G.A. Davis (Eds.), *Handbook of gifted education*. (pp. 43–53). Boston, MA: Allyn and Bacon.

Strop, J., & Goldman, D. (2002). The affective side: Emotional issues of twice-exceptional students. *Understanding Our Gifted*. 28–29. Retrieved: http://sengifted.org/archives/articles/the-affective-side-emotional-issues-of-twice-exceptional-students

Szabos, J. (1989). Note the difference. *Challenge Magazine*. 34. Retrieved: http://www.tag-tenn.org/comparison.html

Szymanski, T., & Shaff, T. (2013). Teacher perspectives regarding gifted diverse students. *Gifted Children*. 14(1), 1–27.

Taibbi, C. (2015). Evaluating gifted programs: Four essential questions. Retrieved: https://www.psychologytoday.com/blog/gifted-ed-guru/201503/evaluating-gifted-programs-four-essential-questions

Teach.com (2016). Become a gifted education teacher. Retrieved: http://teach.com/become-a-gifted-education-teacher

Tomlinson, C.A. (2001). Differentiated instruction in the regular classroom: Why does it matter? What would it look like? *Understanding Our Gifted*. 14(1), 3–6.

Tomlinson, C.A. (2008). *The differentiated school, making revolutionary changes in teaching and learning*. Alexandria, VA: Association for Supervision and Curriculum Development.

Tomlinson, C.A. (n.d.). What it means to teach gifted learners well. Retrieved: https://www.nagc.org/resources-publications/gifted-education-practices/what-it-means-teach-gifted-learners-well

U.S. Department of Education (2004). Title IX, General provisions, p. 388, definition 22. Retrieved: http://www2.ed.gov/policy/elsec/leg/esea02/pg107.html

VanTassel-Baska, J. (2003). *Curriculum planning and design for gifted learners*. Denver, CO: Love Publishing.

Vialle, W., & Tischler, K. (2009). Gifted students' perceptions of the characteristics of effective teachers. In D. Wood (Ed.), *The gifted challenge: Challenging the gifted.* (pp. 115–124). Merrylands, Australia: NSWAGTC Inc. Retrieved: http://ro.uow.edu.au/cgi/viewcontent.cgi?article=2047&context=edupapers

Virginia Advisory Committee for the Education of the Gifted (2013), Educational opportunities for gifted students at the high school level. Retrieved: http://www.doe.virginia.gov/instruction/gifted_ed/opportunities_for_gifted_at_high_school.pdf

Walden, S.L. (2015). What teachers of gifted students should know and be able to do! Retrieved: https://mindworxedu.com/2015/04/11/what-teachers-of-gifted-students-should-know/

Wilderdom (2005). What different I.Q. scores mean. Retrieved: http://www.wilderdom.com/intelligence/IQUnderstandingInterpreting.html

Willard-Holt, C. (n.d.). Evaluation of gifted programs. *PAGE bulletin. Pennsylvania Association for Gifted Education.* Retrieved: http://www.giftedpage.org/docs/bulletins/PageBulletinEvaluation.pdf

Williams, A. (2003). The social and emotional needs of gifted individuals (book review, chapt. 7). *Davidson Institute for Talent Development.* Retrieved: http://www.ditd.org/Cybersource/record.aspx?sid=11093&scat=902&stype=110

Winebrenner, S. (2012). *Teaching gifted kids in today's classroom: Strategies and techniques every teacher can use.* Minneapolis, MN: Free Spirit.

Wolpert-Gawron, H. (2014). Debunking myths about gifted students. Retrieved: http://www.edutopia.org/blog/debunking-myths-about-gifted-students-heather-wolpert-gawron

Wormeli, R. (2006). *Fair isn't always equal: Assessing & grading in the differentiated classroom.* Portland, ME: Stenhouse.

Zirkle, P.A. (2005). *The law on gifted education.* National Research Center on the Gifted and Talented. Retrieved: http://files.eric.ed.gov/fulltext/ED505480.pdf

Index

About the Author

Audrey M. Quinlan, Professor of Education. D.Ed., M.Ed., B.S., Indiana University of Pennsylvania. Curriculum Supervisory Certificate and Principal Certificate, Indiana University of Pennsylvania.

Audrey M. Quinlan holds supervisory, principal, and teacher certifications in elementary education and has taught in both public and parochial schools. She has also served as an elementary/middle school principal and has conducted workshops on Creating Scoring Rubrics as an Assessment Guide, Storytelling, Conflict Resolution, and Learning to Learn. She has published articles in *The Kappan, Horn Book, Principal*, and *Education Digest*, and is the author of *A Complete Guide to Rubrics: Assessment made Easy for Teachers of K-College.*

Dr. Quinlan recently retired as the Chair of the Division of Education and Graduate Program Director at Seton Hill University in Greensburg, Pennsylvania, where she currently teaches a graduate course in gifted education and supervises student teachers. Prior to retirement in 2015, she was elected as "Professor of the Year" and taught methods courses in math and language arts. Her scholarly interests include assessment, conflict resolution, middle level teacher certification, and gifted education.

She and her husband Tim have two adult children and three grandsons and enjoy spending time on the beach in Rodanthe, NC.